Invisible Faces and Hidden Stories

Studies in Public and Applied Anthropology

General Editors: **Sarah Pink**, Monash University, Australia; and **Simone Abram**, Durham University

The value of anthropology to public policy, business and third sector initiatives is increasingly recognized, not least due to significant innovations in the discipline. The books published in this series offer important insight into these developments by examining the expanding role of anthropologists practicing their discipline outside academia as well as exploring the ethnographic, methodological and theoretical contribution of anthropology, within and outside academia, to issues of public concern.

Recent volumes:

Volume 12
Invisible Faces and Hidden Stories: Narratives of Vulnerable Populations and Their Caregivers
Edited by Cecilia Sem Obeng and Samuel Gyasi Obeng

Volume 11
Theoretical Scholarship and Applied Practice
Edited by Sarah Pink, Vaike Fors and Tom O'Dell

Volume 10
Witches and Demons: A Comparative Perspective on Witchcraft and Satanism
Jean La Fontaine

Volume 9
Media, Anthropology and Public Engagement
Edited by Sarah Pink and Simone Abram

Volume 8
Public Anthropology in a Borderless World
Edited by Sam Beck and Carl A. Maida

Volume 7
Up, Down, and Sideways: Anthropologists Trace the Pathways of Power
Edited by Rachael Stryker and Roberto J. González

Volume 6
Adventures in Aidland: The Anthropology of Professionals in International Development
Edited by David Mosse

Volume 5
Ethnography and the Corporate Encounter: Reflections on Research in and of Corporations
Edited by Melissa Cefkin

Volume 4
Visual Interventions: Applied Visual Anthropology
Edited by Sarah Pink

Volume 3
Fire in the Dark: Telling Gypsiness in North East England
Edited by Sarah Buckler

For a full volume listing, please see the series page on our website:
https://www.berghahnbooks.com/series/public-applied-anthropology

Invisible Faces and Hidden Stories

Narratives of Vulnerable Populations and Their Caregivers

Edited by

Cecilia Sem Obeng and Samuel Gyasi Obeng

berghahn
NEW YORK · OXFORD
www.berghahnbooks.com

First published in 2021 by

Berghahn Books

www.berghahnbooks.com

© 2021, 2025 Cecilia Sem Obeng and Samuel Gyasi Obeng
First paperback edition published in 2025

All rights reserved. Except for the quotation of short passages for the purposes of criticism and review, no part of this book may be reproduced in any form or by any means, electronic or mechanical, including photocopying, recording, or any information storage and retrieval system now known or to be invented, without written permission of the publisher.

Library of Congress Cataloging-in-Publication Data

Names: Obeng, Cecilia Sem, editor. | Obeng, Samuel Gyasi, editor.
Title: Invisible Faces and Hidden Stories: Narratives of Vulnerable Populations and Their Caregivers / edited by Cecilia Sem Obeng and Samuel Gyasi Obeng.
Description: New York: Berghahn Books, 2021. | Series: Studies in Public and Applied Anthropology; volume 12 | Includes bibliographical references and index.
Identifiers: LCCN 2020040632 (print) | LCCN 2020040633 (ebook) | ISBN 9781789209334 (hardback) | ISBN 9781789209341 (ebook)
Subjects: LCSH: People with social disabilities—Medical care—United States. | Social medicine—United States. | Social work with people with social disabilities—United States. | Physician and patient—United States. | Medical personnel—United States.
Classification: LCC RA418.5.S63 I48 2021 (print) | LCC RA418.5.S63 (ebook) | DDC 362.4—dc23
LC record available at https://lccn.loc.gov/2020040632
LC ebook record available at https://lccn.loc.gov/2020040633

British Library Cataloguing in Publication Data

A catalogue record for this book is available from the British Library

ISBN 978-1-78920-933-4 hardback
ISBN 978-1-80539-733-5 paperback
ISBN 978-1-80539-924-7 epub
ISBN 978-1-78920-934-1 web pdf

https://doi.org/10.3167/9781789209334

To those whose faces society turns away from,
and whose stories society pretends and hopes do not exist.
May we learn to acknowledge the invisible faces and appreciate the
wisdom their voices carry. Maybe we need listening-ears so that when
push comes to shove, we will hear and act accordingly.

CONTENTS

Prologue *Samuel Gyasi Obeng*	viii
Acknowledgements	xii
Introduction *Cecilia Sem Obeng and Samuel Gyasi Obeng*	1
Chapter 1. 'Foxes Have Dens but I Am Homeless': On the Lived Experiences of a Homeless Man and His Social Worker *Hannah Kelling*	19
Chapter 2. Living with Ataxia: Nancy's and Lisa's Perspectives *Cassie Kresnye*	45
Chapter 3. Discovering Unspoken Communication: Lived Experiences of a Deaf Person and His Doctor *Mackenzie Jones*	66
Chapter 4. Narratives of Two Immigrant Women about Their Lived Experiences in the United States *Dema Kittaneh*	92
Chapter 5. Living as Black and Brown: Culture and Identity on Holistic Health *Kourtney Ayanna Dorqual Byrd*	115
Conclusion *Samuel Gyasi Obeng and Cecilia Sem Obeng*	133
Epilogue *Samuel Gyasi Obeng*	141
Index	143

Prologue

Samuel Gyasi Obeng

We followed these phenomenal human beings for months and years
Our love for them grew in leaps and bounds over time
Our initial meetings consisted of mere greetings
Followed, sometimes, by smiles
Followed, always, by walking past them as if to say:
They may not be ready to talk!

We had obtained permission to learn about them from the powers that be;
Those employed to ensure our work was appropriate and legitimate
And in compliance with 'Whosoevers' Laws!
One after the other we gained the storytellers' Trust!
With Trust came Acceptance
And with Acceptance came Readiness to Share!
And Share, they Did!
Even if interspersed with Hesitations, Various forms of Silence,
Sobbing, and Determined Bravery!

The more we listened,
The more we realized how foolish society had become!
The more an irresponsible Web society had woven around itself!
The more Monitor-Lizard-Like Ears and Hearing we, as a people, have
    Acquired!
We don't hear because we are hard of hearing
We don't hear because we assume their Stories Offer Nothing to Society
We don't hear because our listening is impaired
And yes,
We don't hear because we just don't care!
As we gathered Courage,
We realized that Courage was not enough!

As we learned to be Patient,
We became conscious of the fact that we needed more than just Patience!
As we readied ourselves for our meetings,
We recognized that we needed more than Skill and Alacrity!
We needed to place ourselves in their camera-angles!
We needed to be in that Web of Constellation,
Which 'combined' them and us into 'we'
And yes,
We needed to be normal since they were Very Normal;
And we were NOT!
And This spoke
And That spoke
And These spoke
And Those spoke
This and That
These and Those

This One Shared a Tear
And That One Shared a Tear
These Shared Tears
And Those Shared Tears

Then we heard stories of neglect, anger, bewilderment, and helplessness!
The stories themselves were pregnant with bravery in dealing with:
> Physical health
> Social health
> Emotional health
> Mental health
> Environmental health
> And yes,
> Financial health!

Affliction with Ataxia
A Condition resulting from failure of the brain to regulate posture
Thereby leaving one with poor coordination and unsteadiness
A Condition that makes it impossible to regulate the strength and
  direction of one's limb movements.

Affliction with Deafness
Rendering the stricken individual with hardness of hearing
A condition that makes some in society think and see one as dumb
A Condition that attracts name-calling and arrogant head-shakes

Affliction with Homelessness
A condition that attracts verbal and physical abuse, and avoidance
A condition that easily and quickly negatively impacts one's emotional and financial health
A condition that removes and distances the 'sufferer' from One and All

Then there was the Affliction with Being an Immigrant!
Seen as Other!
Seen as a Minority!
Viewed outside of the Mainstream
Respect taken away,
Distress 'given' in full
Views not Welcome!
Questioned about *When You Will Go Back Home*!
Unwelcome!
Unwanted!
Viewed by some as a Common Criminal!
Viewed by others as a Parasite,
Viewed as Infesting our polity
Waiting to be gotten rid of!
Forced to be Endowed with 'Patience'
Forced to be Educated, Trained, and 'Helped' by the Know-Alls
Conditions that lead to poor nutritional choices leading to Obesity
Worsening physical and emotional health,
And a Deep, Deep, Depression!

The stories of those 'Afflicted' with Blackness and Brownness,
Their stories, not different from those of the Immigrants!
They were 'Other' and viewed as Such!
People who cared about them advised them during adolescence,
To behave in a particular way to Survive
And not get killed by those in Law Enforcement employed to protect them!
Despite being highly Educated,
They had to be careful of the Mainstream in order to Survive,
And pass their genes on to the next generation of Blackness and Brownness.
Their unique Culture and Identity negatively impacted their Health
Some had nightmares
Others had anxieties and phobias
That kept them in environments and ecologies where they felt Society wanted them to Be!

These and many others were the stories we heard
These and many others were the tales told unto Us
These and many others were the narratives we chronicled!
From faces that had hitherto been invisible
And from those whose stories had hitherto been imperceptible!
Faces that must be seen!
Voices that must be heard!
Stories that humanize the faceless
Faces that tell us to open our ears
To listen and act appropriately!

Acknowledgements

We acknowledge with thanks people who shared their stories with us. They may have asked to remain anonymous, but their stories unearthed their 'hidden' innermost feelings and their desire to be heard. May those who have ears hear, act and bring them relief.

We are most grateful to the three anonymous reviewers for their comments and suggestions, and to colleagues who perused this volume at different stages and offered professional advice. The reviews, editorial comments and criticisms helped to sharpen the content, organization and mechanics of this book. 'No one has monopoly over wisdom; neither does anyone have monopoly of knowledge' (Akan-Ghanaian proverb). The wisdom and knowledge provided by these professionals helped to shape the scope and quality of this book.

INTRODUCTION

Cecilia Sem Obeng and Samuel Gyasi Obeng

> Those big ears hear nothing because they care less about us.
> —Akan proverb

The narratives in this volume range over health concerns: physical, social, cultural, spiritual, financial, emotional, mental and environmental. They also reflect and refract the sociopolitical ecology in which vulnerable populations operate and, in addition, modulate both research and discourse ecologies. The narratives unearth an imbalance between the pivotal role played by the voices in the creation of wealth in the United States, the neglect, sometimes, of their unique health needs, and their plea to be heard in order to obtain optimal health.

An important theme that runs through the gamut of the narratives is the devastating incongruence between voice, ear and action. Society gives the impression that it is listening to the plight of vulnerable populations, but when push comes to shove, it refuses to hear and hence takes no action to better the lives and the lot of such populations. These vulnerable lives, we learned, will be changed for the better if society listened and acted accordingly.

The privilege of listening to the vulnerable populations' stories brings companionship between the participants and the chapter contributors. In particular, the researchers who contributed to this volume learned through the narratives about the researched population. This was done through relationships via intentional personal interactions and methodological strategies that helped to augment work on public health and medical discourse given the richness of the narratives in providing information about the health needs of the vulnerable populations and how they accessed healthcare. Specifically, the narratives provide the reader with the opportunity to learn about how vulnerable populations deal with their various dimensions of health and the ups and downs in their daily struggles to seek optimal health. As we 'listen' to the hitherto-muted voices via the contributors' transcripts, we hear exasperation and squirming; we observe chortling and cheering, as well as enthusiasm and agonizing. Their voices give in and then cheer up, address themes of neglect by society, of societies' responsibility to care for the vulnerable and of the associated anger at a nation's blindness towards its citizens' sufferings. We also hear about the power of the human spirit to overcome adversity, and the love of family and healthcare providers, among others, in mitigating the negative and harmful effects of the problems encountered by the vulnerable populations. We learn about public hostility and stereotyping endured by vulnerable populations, such as the homeless, and their suggestions about how to deal with them.

To enable us to understand the stories told by our studied participants, we have, in the following chapters, placed the narrators at the centre-stage of the discourse ecology. This helps to avoid any form of marginalization and further muting of their voices. Context is provided for each narrative and care is taken not to distort the narrators' intended meanings. Indeed, the narrators provide explications of their ideas as well as questions posed to them by the researchers when necessary. Thus, not only are the narrators generous with their time, they are equally generous with the synthesis and analyses of the facts they provide.

Given that the narrators' own elucidation and explication of their lived experiences and social actions are grounded in their own experiences and thought processes, we believe that any attempt by the chapter contributors to undertake any further synthesis and analysis will be redundant and unnecessary; such contributor elucidations are therefore, for the most part, avoided. In effect, the storytellers are not mere narrators; their stories unearth, explain and discuss who they are, what they are going through, and ways of solving their problems. Thus, via metalanguage, they position the reader or society in a way that makes the content of their stories easy to comprehend.

Consequently, the narratives are presented in exactly the same content and style that the narrators told them. No syntactic, semantic or pragmatic changes or errors have been corrected and no content has been modified. The punctuation marks used correlate with narrators' phonetic output, such as pausing and prolongation, as carefully and as accurately as the authors are able to transcribe them. Given that all clarifications and explications of facts are carried out by the narrators themselves, sometimes on their own accord and at other times when prompted with a probe, it is fair to state that the data are authentic.

The contributors focused on specific individuals and spent time undertaking extensive interviews that enabled the studied participants to present their stories in an unconstrained way. The interviews were conducted unidirectionally, thereby enabling the interviewees to also ask questions if they chose to. There was little to no interruption whenever the narrators had the floor or their turn.

The knowledge to be gained from this volume in general, and from the narratives in particular, has wide tentacles. There is health information, especially the narrators' accounts of how they view their physical, social, emotional, mental, environmental, financial and other forms of health. There is also information about how they accessed healthcare and its associated problems, society's attitude towards them and how that impacts their emotional and social lives and health, their support systems and networks, and their resilience in the face of discrimination, domination and exclusionist ideologies. The narrators' hidden concerns and wishes are rooted in objective reality, not in ignorance. They sometimes observe their negative and positive liberties (Berlin 1969; Obeng 2018, 2020) being intruded upon daily by the powers that be with no one ready to listen to them. Through their narratives, they seek a restoration of these liberties. This is despite the fact that government and/or other institutions 'hold them hostage' because of their being physically challenged, being homeless, being an immigrant or being a minority. They seek their positive liberty by asking to be allowed to participate in their own affairs and in the affairs of their communities.

Their challenges (physical, emotional, social and financial, among others) are different and unique, yet one thesis is common: they want to be heard and given an opportunity to function as normal human beings and as authentic members of their communities. Whether it is being Black, suffering from ataxia, being hearing impaired, being homeless, being an immigrant or being a healthcare provider, these knowledgeable and very reasonable human beings reject 'otherness' and seek to be part of the mainstream and given an opportunity to contribute their quota to the gamut of society and to nation building, and not to be viewed as helpless freeloaders or, in some cases, privileged healthcare and social services providers.

The chapter summaries below prepare us for the informative narratives and elucidations in Chapters 1–5. The final chapter, the conclusion, provides a summary of the salient points of the volume and a brief conclusion.

Chapter Summaries

Chapter 1 by Hannah Kelling deals with the lived experiences of a homeless person, Mark, and of a person (a caregiver) who works with homeless people, respectively. In first part of the chapter, Mark narrates his lived experiences as a homeless person of between two and five years, and how that makes him see Hannah as being of good fortune and privilege. He speaks about how he became homeless, something he described as being by choice since it afforded him an opportunity to see his son who lived with his (Mark's) divorced wife. Thus, as Kelling rightly hints, Mark's homelessness was motivated by choice, but even more so by his love for family and his willingness to be close to them, even if this would make him homeless. He explains his encounter with addiction to drugs and alcohol, being incarcerated every now and then, his wife's disrespect for him as a result of his homelessness and inability to hold a job, how desperation drives him and other homeless persons to deal in drugs in order to make money to stay afloat, and how he tries many times to put his life back together, as well as the hurdles he has faced as a result of unpaid bills among other things. Kelling's rendition of Mark's willingness to 'volunteer' information as being characteristic of someone whose words 'had been waiting just below the surface for a long time, waiting for the opportunity to come forward' testifies to the extent to which this hitherto imperceptive voice was looking for an opportunity to be heard with the view to finding a solution to his unique crisis.

Mark's narrative unveils a policy deficiency in Indiana: that of not having homeless shelters known to him in Orange County or in any other county in Southern Indiana, except perhaps in Evansville. His concern points to the need to inform and educate the homeless community in Southern Indiana about the presence of such facilities in order to lessen their burden and help them seek shelter if need be.

Mark shares his daily routines, his personal experience with housing officials and how his unique situation makes him unqualified to receive housing. His cynicism about the system, which he saw as rigged against the homeless, was made manifest – something that made him see the police, the city, county officials and everyone else for that matter as being in cahoots against him and his homeless friends. Indeed, he viewed the police as stalking and profiling the homeless. He ends his narrative with a call for structures to be put in place for everyone to own a house so as to enable them to function as normal human beings.

Mark's story no doubt opens up a pathway into an unspeakable but real situation in American social structure and organization, deviance and control, an unfair resource allocation, and how that ends up throwing some people off the visible grid or medium, thereby making the faces of the negatively affected, invisible and consequently their voices imperceptible.

The second narrative is that of Andrea, a caseworker with the Peace Shelter Center. Andrea narrates (to Hannah Kelling) her two-year experience regarding her normal work routine of assisting the homeless. Kelling describes Andrea as having a rare persona that conveys conflicting qualities of sweetness and toughness, as well as calmness and self-assurance in the midst of chaos and dissonance associated with her work.

Regarding her motivations for pursuing a career in casework and her own personal theories about why homelessness exists, Andrea delved into her previous experience of working for people with disabilities, managing group homes and working with clients who had very severe behavioural issues. She also spoke about her position in the Rapid Rehousing programme and how all this impacted her professional and personal lives. Andrea's love for personal interaction with the homeless, especially regarding their most vulnerable state, made her learn more about the people she and her social work colleagues assisted in particular and about homelessness in general. She describes the Center's target of serving a minimum of twenty people a day (even though some days they saw forty or more) and its provision of housing and/or financial assistance to enable people gain access to housing. Andrea's success as a caseworker at the Peace Center is captured by the strategy she adopted, a stance that emphasized the importance of and need for a carefully planned and administered empathy, as well as the fact that: 'Too little, and you fail to connect with your client. Too much, and you may unravel yourself.' Andrea thus calls for a balance between keeping one's sanity and professional etiquette, while at the same time making every effort to connect with one's clients.

Using her own lived experience with family members who went through addiction and housing uncertainty and how that impacted her, Andrea elucidates such problems as clients' pride or unwillingness to share the unique stories leading to their homelessness. She also explains the Peace Center's inability to deal with detoxification, which results in referring clients to other relevant centres. All the above, Andrea's notes, are some of the barriers that the centre had to deal with. She notes how empathy causes burnout in social workers and case managers, and the need to sometimes resort to sympathy rather than empathy. She elucidates the complexities associated with health insurance and how co-pays and high-premium payments all negatively impact the homeless community, as well as how, on some occasions, different individuals and agencies help mitigate and solve this problem for the homeless. She also discusses how huge medical bills, wanton arrests of the homeless by law-enforcement officers, and a lack of effective and efficient support systems contribute to housing instability, leading to homelessness. Furthermore, she explains the preponderance of mental health issues among the homeless population and how this is viewed and dealt with. She ends by calling on other caseworkers and society to provide emotional support to this community and to help them with navigating the complex healthcare services that may be available to them.

Chapter 2 by Cassie Kresnye deals with two individuals, Nancy and Lisa, both of whom suffer from ataxia; a condition associated with poor coordination and unsteadiness due to the brain's failure to regulate posture as well as the strength and direction of limb movements. In the first narrative, Kresnye 'invites' her readers into the lived experience of Nancy with regard to the debilitating effects of the disease on her balance and the way she walks, especially her inability to walk straight, her unpredictable falls and how her use of Rollator and a cane sometimes help mitigate her falls. Nancy educates Kresnye (and hence the readers of this volume) on the time of her diagnosis with ataxia, the causes of the disease, the various texts, contexts and steps that went into her diagnosis of the disease, and the fact that the disease can be managed, not cured. She also discusses the various physical and neurological activities associated with the disease, her participation in drug and medical procedure trials and studies aimed at helping her get well, as well as support groups in which she had had to participate in order to stay healthy. Nancy expounded the extent to which age and other environmental factors (such as the home environment, crowded environments, etc.) impacted her ability to participate in the much-needed physical and neurological activities aimed at helping her manage the disease. She also allows us into her personal experience with her mother's own fight with ataxia and how she dealt with her own diagnosis regarding disease management. She also educates us about how she broke the bad news to her immediate family (her husband, daughter and son) and how the family jointly dealt with the emotional valence and social trauma associated with such bad news. She also shared how the family worked with medical personnel to manage the disease itself.

There is no doubt that Nancy's story is emblematic of someone with courage and determination to survive, and even overcome adversity. She turned her unique situation into a teachable construct by assisting society in understanding the disease and in helping others to get an education. It is not surprising that she ends the interview with the expression: 'There's a lot of hope.' Indeed, there is a lot of hope if her voice, a voice that explicates her unique personal experience, is listened to and if her concerns are dealt with.

The object of the second part of Chapter 2 is Kresnye's presentation of her interaction with Lisa, a woman in her fifties who is also an ataxia patient, and her elucidation and elaboration of Lisa's lived experience with the disease. Lisa discusses who her caregivers were (with her husband being the main one) and the steps and health issues (such as blaming her lack of coordination on her knee and hence having the doctors do the knee surgery that she went through before learning she had ataxia. She takes us through her childhood experiences, her adulthood journey and the eventual diagnosis of the disease. She also discusses her experiences with different doctors in various specialized areas, especially those in neurology, and the various tests and procedures that were recommended to her. Furthermore, she takes us through the various support groups she learned about and those in which she got involved, as well as the impact they had had on her disease management. Her use of metaphors such as 'I like to think ataxia is like a broken arm' points to her linguistic and communicative prowess in explicating the labelling, finger-pointing and sometimes avoidance that people suffering from various diseases must deal with daily. She informs us how joining support groups and leaving one's ecology to interact with others in different ecologies helped her to deal with her disease. In particular, she explains how knowledge and entertainment that are shared and enjoyed in the various support groups helped to lift the burden of stress and entrapment associated with staying in a solitary ecology where one is ensnared in the same place without respite.

Lisa also talks about her real fears, such as the possibility of falling down stairs or of going to crowded places and how she deals with them. Her story, like that of Nancy, is one of a test and contest of willpower, of survival and of an understanding that there is hope at the end of the struggles and difficult tunnels that ataxia sufferers must navigate.

In the first part of Chapter 3, Mackenzie Jones presents the narrative of Trip, a gastroenterologist whose passion was to provide healthcare to his patients. Trip happened to be Jones' doctor, so getting him to participate in the interview was not very difficult; in fact, it was Trip who encouraged Jones to share her interests and goals for 'changing the world', so Jones' interest in patients with communication disorders such as deaf/hard-of-hearing populations coincided directly into Trip's clinical interest, since he was caring for patients, some of whom had communication disorders. Trip could fingerspell his name and was also vaguely familiar with American Sign Language (ASL).

Jones notes that her goal when interviewing Trip was to understand the communication strategies actually used in a hospital or a doctor's office when a patient is deaf and to explore the experience of a physician who may not be used to working with Deaf people on a regular basis. Jones prefaces her presentation of the narrative by elucidating the rationale behind establishing the Americans with Disabilities Act (ADA) and what Titles II and III say about nondiscrimination against those with communication disorders, as well as the need for government-run and nongovernmental organizations to consider their preferences for communication aids in order to ensure the highest quality of care. She disambiguates the expressions 'Deaf', 'deaf' and 'hard of hearing' by helping her readers to understand 'deaf' and 'hard of hearing' (the medical condition) and 'Deaf' (the culture of the Deaf world).

In the interview itself, Trip mentions his background growing up in a home with a doctor parent – a situation that drew him into medicine and subsequently impacted his choice of specialization/residency. He also mentions how he was introduced to ASL and talks about there being someone who knows ASL (an interpreter) and who helped with translation/interpretation at the clinic. He describes 'generic' classes that he took in Medical School on working with patients with disabilities, which were mainly done without actual patients being brought into class to help give them hands-on experience. He lucidly describes his strategies with hearing impaired patients; these include raising his voice, sitting in front of them for them to read his lips and using ASL if necessary. He also explains how letters are often used as modes of communication to refer patients to other specialists and to invite the clients back if the need arises to explain specific conditions to them in follow-up sessions. He notes the difficulties nurses and other personnel have in communicating with them and mentions the frequency of encounter with hearing-impaired clients. He also cites specific cases where procedures have to be carried out on his patients and the overall communicative events that take place before and after surgery with such clients. He notes also how a Video Relay System (VRS) and computer monitors on rolling tables are used for interpreters in the hospital if they (the doctors/hospitals) are the ones who provide the interpreter. Also, he acknowledges the fact that more can be done to improve the communication between hard-of-hearing patients and their healthcare providers at the hospitals. Jones calls for improvements in communicative modes in the medical discourse ecology to ensure effective communication and patient-physician satisfaction.

The object of the second section of Jones' chapter is a presentation and an elucidation of the narrative of Adam, a deaf (hearing-impaired) patient who is a professor of ASL. Jones elucidates how Adam uses cordial interlocution with his students to set the scene for his class each morning. She recalls how Adam helped her improve her ASL and her understanding of the culture of the Deaf community. She also explains how he assisted her in finding an interpreter during data collection and synthesis. In particular, the Jones–Adam interaction provides insights into techniques in collecting data from the Deaf community and into how an interpreter functions within the deaf discourse ecology.

According to Jones, Adam's story provides instances of positive and negative interactions with healthcare providers. It also provides ideas for providing and ensuring a more equitable healthcare system. Furthermore, given that Adam used ASL, Jones draws our attention to the fact that the narrative transcripts are based on the interpreter's rendition of Adam's ASL. Also, taking into consideration the problems associated with translation in general and ASL in particular, she acknowledges the possibility of some communicative facets being lost in translation and interpretation.

In the narrative itself, Adam explicates his encounter with doctors, how communicative frames are established and employed in the management of the health discourse, the problems encountered with sound and prosody articulation (production), including various forms of lip aperture and interpretation, and solutions found to ensure the achievement of successful health communication outcomes and goals.

Adam also provides us with a glimpse of the nature of the discourse at the doctor's office reception and how trust and authenticity are established between a client and the office staff before a client is allowed into a doctor's office. He alludes to the fact that it is the fight for civil rights that has led to the establishment of Deaf people being afforded the right to see doctors.

Moreover, he provides an account of his childhood, how his parents detected he was hearing impaired and the steps they took to educate him. He also provides a fascinating insight into the linguistic structure of, and communicative strategies, in ASL and explains clearly why ASL is not English, but a unique language with its own unique syntax and pragmatics. He elucidates this further by explaining the centrality of facial expressions, gestures (body language, lip aperture, hand shapes, hand movements and fingerspelling), gaze and proximity in ASL interactions. He speaks about his college days, pointing out his initial majors of interest and how he settled on a B.S. in construction management. He also provides an insight into his search for employment and how that took him to New York, where Deaf people are viewed as high risk, despite the Americans with Disabilities Act, which protects people like him from employment discrimination. He eventually ended up as a professor of ASL after completing a master's degree.

Furthermore, Adam talks about support from his parents and siblings when he was growing up, and how he wished advocacy had been part of his early education. He also mentions the challenges he experiences as an adult, including healthcare affordability, the fact that he had to live on social security at some point, not having health insurance, and the negative attitude and stigma attached to being deaf. He describes the 'horrible' and 'horrendous' nature of certain hospitals due to doctors and nurses not responding immediately to requests and the absence of interpreters at some clinics. He also explains how hospitals now use VRS (to provide an equivalent to telephone services for deaf and hard-of-hearing people) and Video Remote Interpreting (to provide interpreting services for many languages) to ensure effective communication between doctors/nurses and their hard-of-hearing clients. He notes that he prefers family members acting as interpreters rather than the use of technology or hospital interpreters if a deaf person's illness is severe, given the emotions associated with illness. He recommends ASL language and Deaf culture training for doctors to create awareness of their unique situation, to increase the doctors' understanding of the Deaf culture and consequently increase the doctors' efficiency in working with the Deaf community.

In Chapter 4, Dema Kittaneh presents the narrative of a Jordanian immigrant Amy living in the United States and shows how her status impacts her health. She prefaces the narrative with a brief review of the literature on migration in general and emigration into the United States in particular. Specifically, she explicates such problems as difficulties speaking and learning English, raising children and helping them succeed in schools, securing work, securing housing, accessing social and economic services, using transportation, and overcoming cultural barriers. She draws on the work of Garrett (2006), who also examines problems of migration and discusses the facts about immigrants being vulnerable due to increased risk for poor physical, psychological and social health outcomes, as well as inadequate healthcare (see also Aday 2001; Flaskerud and Winslow 1998). Amy, a fifty-year-old former Jordanian banker, came to the United States at the age of twenty-three by chance and became an immigrant without the intention of permanently settling in the country. Amy, according to Kittaneh, went from being a banker in her home country to becoming a housewife and mother of three after settling in the United States, a situation that, according to Kittaneh, negatively impacted her physical, mental, social, financial and spiritual health.

Amy, Kittaneh notes, spoke about the open-mindedness and educated status of the people of Bloomington, Indiana, and the large and growing presence of international students and transnational people making it a hospitable place to live. Also, Kittaneh quotes Amy as speaking about the 'lazy' lifestyle in the United States, which she felt could potentially affect her children in the long run. She saw as problematic the practice whereby people refrained from cooking and ate mainly from restaurants, something that she thought negatively affected their health. In terms of physical health, Kittaneh quotes Amy as noting that Bloomington has gyms, the YMCA (to which she signed her children up to be members), swimming pools, parks and everything needed for one to maintain good physical health, and consequently to become confident as well as being part of the community. Amy's children volunteered in such organizations as Habitat for Humanity, Riley Hospital and Key Club as part of being authentic members of the Bloomington community.

On the kind of activities that influenced Amy, Kittaneh points to the fact that despite taking a walk with her husband on a regular basis, Amy gained weight because after childbirth she resorted to eating fast food, sitting and watching TV. An important fact brought up in Amy's narrative was that whereas in Jordan people 'monitor' one another's weight and appearance and openly question individuals if they notice any dramatic changes such as excessive weight gain, in the US people mind their own business and refrain from openly commenting on the bodily appearance of others. This cultural difference, Amy notes, may have contributed to her gaining weight, since no one drew her attention to it. According to Kittaneh, upon Amy's return to Jordan, she was openly criticized for not taking care of her body and becoming obese, which made her feel embarrassed. The fact that she was diagnosed as prediabetic as well as her motivation to be healthy made her determined to lose weight. Among other steps, he cut out junk food, mainly ate home-cooked meals and took daily walks in order to lose weight.

Amy credited the US health system with providing customized strategies for keeping people healthy by referring them to a dietician for help. In her case, she also had lap-band surgery and lost 70 pounds. An important message she has for others is for them to take their health into their own hands and work to improve it. The issue of health insurance in general, and the fact that most poor or poorly paid individuals have no health insurance in particular, came up in her narrative. She elucidates how the Affordable Care Act (Obamacare) came as a reprieve for her family. She praises Bloomington doctors for being nice, nondiscriminatory and professional without necessarily looking at how much money one has. Her narrative, Kittaneh notes, also touches on her husband's health problems, which include being overweight, having high cholesterol, cardiovascular problems, diabetes and high blood pressure, as well as suffering two heart attacks. Obamacare, she re-emphasizes, met their health needs.

Amy's narrative ends on a positive note about her family's improved financial health, which involved her and her husband starting a new grocery business and feeling successful despite the physical burden of working from 10:30 AM to 7:30 PM each day. The narrative ends with an emphasis on how the physical, financial and social dimensions of her health have improved and with a suggestion made to public health professionals to advocate for health policies that can help improve the health of vulnerable populations.

In the second section of the chapter, Kittaneh writes about the health experiences of another immigrant, Hama, who hailed from northern Nigeria and who, like Amy, was a housewife. Hama emigrated to the United States at the age of nineteen as a result of getting married and had lived in

Bloomington for twenty-two years by the time the interview took place. She had five children, aged 21, 19, 14, 11 and 4 months. Kittaneh discusses the attempt by Hama's family to move back to Nigeria in 2015 and how the activities of the terrorist group Boko Haram made it impossible for them to live peacefully, and consequently forced them to move back to the United States after only six months in Nigeria.

Hama spoke about her financial health, especially about being able to work and make some money. Her ability to work gave her confidence and satisfaction for the first time in life. However, she quit working after becoming pregnant. She also recounts that in the 1970s because of discrimination her husband could not find a job. However, things have changed over the years, making it easier for him in this respect. She noted further that the change in attitude towards Black people in Bloomington has improved her family's financial health, making it possible for them to pay for accommodation, health and food, and to even have some savings.

Hama had no medical issues and praised the US environmental health system as well as the overall medical system compared to that of Nigeria – something that she said had benefited her children. For example, an observation of Kittaneh's transcripts indicates the absence of malaria in the United States as being a big difference between healthcare access in the United States and Nigeria. Hama condemns the Nigerian medical system, sometimes harshly. It is important to note that even though some of her examples – such as the same medication (including dosage) being given to adults and children– could be called into question, the fact that she makes this observation is noteworthy. In particular, we observe from Kittaneh's transcripts how Hama speaks about the persistent use of injections to treat people suffering from all kinds of illnesses and how nurses instead of doctors prescribe medication. Hama notes that she was unhappy with this state of affairs in Nigeria. Her narrative briefly touched on dental healthcare in the United States and how her children had benefited from it. She notes that moving to the United State has been a positive move for her in terms of her health, and she credits her good health to her engagement in physical activity, especially exercising (walking).

In terms of safety, Hama considered Nigeria to be safer than the United States (Bloomington) in terms of taking a walk, since most of the people you meet when you take a walk in Nigeria are known to you. She attributes the relative safety in Bloomington to people abiding by the rules set by the city.

Regarding the social and emotional health of her children, Hama notes that her children were not affected negatively either emotionally or socially, except for one incident that involved other children telling her daughter to take off her Hijab (headscarf), something that made her daughter feel awkward. This apparent bullying stopped after her daughter's involvement in a TV programme. On the subject of physical health, Hama mentions that such activities as swimming, running and playing basketball help to keep her children fit.

On education, Hama spoke about the poor educational system in northern Nigeria brought about by teachers' incompetence in English, the official language of instruction. She also spoke about her difficulty in understanding American English when she first came to the United States. She commended and attributed her children's educational success to her husband, who she said was dedicated to the children's education, assisted them with their homework and also helped them to read and learn English.

In relation to her marriage, Hama spoke about the socioemotional advantage of living in the United States, since wives and husbands support each other, unlike in Nigeria, where the husband barely comes home and the wife is stuck with the children at home, a situation that negatively affects the wife and children's emotional and social health.

On the subject of spiritual health, Kittaneh quotes Hama as saying that she does things that are consistent with her religion, but not necessarily with her Hausa (Nigerian) culture. Unlike her husband, who adapted to American culture because his friends were African American, she had only Arab friends, thus making it difficult for her to understand and adopt such American cultural mores as those relating to birthday celebrations.

Another aspect of socioemotional health noted by Hama related to clothing or lack thereof, especially seeing American women as 'naked' because of how little they wear. This, she noted, made her angry with her husband, leading her to question his integrity. Specifically, she blamed her husband for taking her for a walk in order to give himself the opportunity to watch 'naked' women. She barred him from watching TV because of what she perceived as 'naked' women on TV. Eventually, she came to accept American clothing culture, despite the exception she took to some of the cultural mores.

In Chapter 5, Kourtney Ayanna Dorqual Byrd examines issues of identity of two Black graduate students, an Afro-Caribbean female and an African American male at Indiana University-Bloomington. Specifically, she collected narratives that revealed how the Black identity of graduate students impacts their health. Via these narratives, she stresses the negative emotional health about being Black in the United States. She notes that Black people in general, and Afro-Caribbean and African Americans in particular, face racial stressors in their daily lives and that these stressors negatively influence their physical, emotional, spiritual and mental health, as well as undermining their attitudes towards their racial identity.

Byrd cites statistics from the US Commission on Civil Rights (2010) and from Indiana University-Bloomington, which showed the relative low enrolment of Black people in higher education (colleges and universities) due to their Black identity.

Byrd prefaces her research participants' narrative with a brief discussion of the Black Graduate Student Association, an organization at Indiana University-Bloomington that is dedicated to promoting and championing the academic, professional, mental and social wellbeing of Black graduate and professional students. Byrd's Black identity group membership made her entry into the researched participants' lives much easier. Even though over thirty people responded to her recruitment email, she selected the first two responders as participants in the study. She uses qualitative methods of research (narrative methodology via interviewing) to understand and present the kind of life experiences that influence one's health and to discover any potential information that will help improve not just the respondents' health, but also that of Black America in general. The only qualification for participating in Byrd's study was, besides being Black and a graduate student or student in the professional school, being eighteen years of age or older. Using two semi-structured interviews, Byrd spoke with each interviewee for between 15 and 30 minutes. She asked about the kind of activities that influenced the respondents' health and about the strategies that helped them deal with any problems that influenced or helped to improve their health. On the question of the activities that influenced her health, Respondent 1 (Interviewee-1) mentioned: (a) sleeping (which she said influenced her thinking –the more sleep she had, the better she could think); (b) hanging out with people in the community for upliftment of one's spirit; (c) being in solitude to refresh one's self; and (d) eating (where she notes that eating the wrong food did not connect body with mind and spirit and also negatively impacted her output).

On the body–mind–soul connection, the respondent noted that she had very bad migraines and that the dining hall food made these worse, since the food was not made with 'love and care'. The food, she noted, lacked the energy that should be there for those who eat it. She would have preferred home-cooked meals made with love and care. She did not see the meals served in the dining halls as 'real' meals; they were not spiritually fulfilling and so caused her to have headaches, to be frustrated and consequently to have a negative impact on her soul. Her energy 'feels off', she noted. She wanted 'cultural' food and spicy food that did not make her sick.

The interviewee reaffirms her need for space (not a shared area that she viewed as often being dirty, filthy and disgusting) to enable her to bake her food and to cook what she considered real food (food that is 'well' and tastes good). She saw baking, aromatherapy and painting as being therapeutic for her because they helped her relax and release tension. Having space to think about herself also relaxed her. Cooking, painting, yoga, going to the gym and cleaning, among other activities, provided extra support for her relaxation and releasing of inner stress (tension). She considers water, sun and being in the community as rejuvenating her body, mind and spirit.

On racial identity, Interviewee 1 talks about being Black, being a woman, being queer and being Afro-Caribbean. She talks about how, in accessing healthcare, her self-work and identity are not seen as a priority unless one was really sick or even dying. She notes that Black people are expected to do more than anyone else to the extent that even if they are sick, they must show up for class to avoid falling into stereotypes set for Black people. For Black students, this situation creates physical presence in the classroom, but emotional and spiritual absence from the classroom – what she refers to as post-traumatic slave syndrome.

To help other people improve upon their health, Interviewee 1 talks about getting to know the constituents and determinants of health and knowing what kind of activity is good for the body. She ends with an important message; 'One cannot be well if one does not know oneself . . . and whether one is willing to sacrifice' to get well.

The object of the second narrative in Byrd's chapter is a presentation and a brief explication of the life story of the second interviewee (Interviewee 2). Interviewee 2 defined health as an equilibrium (a state of wellness where everything is in proper alignment and function) and effectiveness in meeting one's needs, and the insurance that one is in the appropriate blood pressure range. He categorizes health as mental health, physical health and the overall wellbeing of an individual.

On the list of activities that influence his health by maintaining balance, Interviewee 2 sees the amount of work and physical activity one has to do as being the most important determinant of maintaining good health. Specifically, he notes that one's capacity to exercise and to eat right and have a job are the most important determinants of activities needed to measure one's state of health.

On how his Black identity impacted his health, Interviewee 2 stresses the negative emotional health about being Black in the United States by noting that Black Americans face racial stressors in their daily lives and that these stressors negatively influence their physical and mental health, as well as undermining their attitudes towards their racial identity.

An important difference between Interviewee 1 and Interviewee 2 is that Interviewee 2 took every opportunity that came his way to ask Byrd questions about her health. For example, he asks Byrd if she had the luxury of free time to work out, an expendable or disposable income to have a gym membership, enough money to purchase health food options and whether she lived in a 'food desert', given that the above-mentioned factors affect one's health. He speaks of work that involves several hours of sitting as going against physical activity and hence physical health, while high-intensity and stressful tasks such as studying as negatively impacting both physical and mental health, as well as one's overall wellbeing. Other activities that influence health, Interviewee 2 argues, are maintaining balance, having enough sleep, not overexerting one's self and managing one's time efficiently, as well as identifying role models and following their health-related guidance. Also mentioned by Interviewee 2 are: (a) seeing a dietician and a mental health therapist; (b) maintaining one's mental and spiritual health; (c) connecting with people who share one's interests and who can talk about the stress they themselves are going through and consequently help one deal with stress; (d) building habits and behaviours necessary for creating long-term optimal health; and (e) reassuring and sustaining ecologies that help nurture and sustain the best possible health outcomes.

Intl-2 laments divisions in the Black community and things that members of the community ought to do to improve their health, but that they are not doing presently. He also explicates perceived and intended identities as well as intersectionality (which he notes was born out of Black feminism and Black womanism) and notes that, if unbalanced, the different identities create distance and barriers. He calls on Black people to choose their most salient identity marker rather than having it imposed on them. This, he notes, is because relegating some of one's identity to the background or leaving out aspects of one's identity leads to unhealthy coping mechanisms, which thus negatively impact one's mental, emotional, spiritual and physical health, given the fact that they could lead to overeating, unhealthy engagement in sex, and overcommitting, among other things.

Regarding suggestions about improving one's health, Interviewee 2 talks about identifying and being aware of one's mental, emotional, spiritual, physical and intellectual health, and what these involve. He also advises people to see a therapist (to see how one is doing mentally), an advisor (about time management) and a dietician (to find out whether what one is eating is right). He ends by recommending Indiana University-Bloomington's Counseling and Psychological Services to Black students, since the people who work there are Black and understand their unique needs.

The conclusion involves a summary of the main points raised in the volume and a few concluding remarks followed by recommendations of our own. We highlight how the interdisciplinary nature of the volume and the entwining of the various disciplines help us understand the plight of vulnerable populations. We also bring out common themes in the narratives – in particular, their provision of a glimpse into the lived experiences of the studied participants, and vulnerable populations in general, from their unique perspectives and spaces. We also emphasize another theme: that of people finding strategies to deal with their unique social and psychological situations and with the physical, social, financial, emotional and environmental dimensions of their health. We note that the content, context and co-text of the narrators' stories are pathways to strong, enduring and successful survival and character-building blocks. Also noted is how the narrators' ability to build supportive families impacts their person, personality, mind, soul and spirit. The homeless, for example, bond with one another as a family and support one another; this helps them deal with some of the physical and emotional difficulties they face on the street.

An important conclusion we draw is that society, government, social work actors, healthcare providers and all stakeholders must pay attention to the participants' narratives because the stories reveal voids in the lives of the participants that need to be filled in order for them to live as normal human beings.

Finally, we highlight the entwining of language, power, ideology, justice, healthcare access and healthcare delivery. We also draw attention to moral lessons, such as the need to provide physical and infrastructural resources for vulnerable populations and the need to provide the deaf with interpreters, as well as to recognize their fight to be heard. We also highlight the struggle of vulnerable populations against racism and xenophobia, and their battle against other forms of discrimination. We point out that in order for society to live up to expectations, the words, 'Life, Liberty, and the pursuit of Happiness' in Thomas Jefferson's Independence Declaration must be seen as relevant, even required, in order to meet the challenge in ensuring optimal health and safety for one and all.

Cecilia Sem Obeng is a tenured Associate Professor in the Department of Applied Health Science at Indiana University-Bloomington's School of Public Health, Bloomington. She is an established scholar in the field of children's health and has published six books. She is the author of over sixty peer-reviewed publications. She has provided over a hundred academic/professional and scientific presentations at conferences and has also been an invited speaker. She has spent several years undertaking community-based research in African American communities and publishing her findings in peer-reviewed journals. She has mentored over fifty students to present papers at national and international conferences.

Samuel Gyasi Obeng is a tenured full Professor of Linguistics at Indiana University-Bloomington. He is also an affiliated faculty of Indiana University-Bloomington's Hutton Honors College and the African Studies Program (which he directed from 2007 to 2015) in the Hamilton Lugar School of Global and International Studies. He has published thirty books, over 150 papers in refereed journals and book chapters, and twenty-five book and article reviews. He was also the editor-in-chief of *Africa Today*, *Issues in Intercultural Communication* and *Issues in Political Discourse Analysis*.

References

Aday, Lu Ann. 2001. *At Risk in America: The Health and Health Care Needs of Vulnerable Populations in the United States*. San Francisco: Jossey-Bass.

Americans with Disabilities Act (Titles II and III). 2019. 'National Network Information Guidance, and Training'. Retrieved 14 May 2020 from https://adata.org/factsheets_en.

Berlin, Isaiah. 1969. *Four Essays on Liberty*. Oxford: Oxford University Press.

Flaskerud, Jacquelyn, and Betty Winslow. 1998. 'Conceptualizing Vulnerable Populations Health-Related Research', *Nursing Research* 47(2): 69–78.

Garrett, Katherine. 2006. *Living in America: Challenges Facing New Immigrants and Refugees*. Robert Wood Johnson Foundation. Retrieved 14 May 2020 from https://www.rwjf.org/en/library/research/2006/08/living-in-america.html.

Jefferson, Thomas. 1776. 'The Declaration of Independence: The Want, Will, and Hopes of the People'. Retrieved 14 May 2020 from http://www.ushistory.org/Declaration/document.

Obeng, Samuel Gyasi. 2020. 'Grammatical Pragmatics: Language, Power and Liberty in African (Ghanaian) Political Discourse', *Discourse and Society* 31(1): 85–104.

———. 2018. 'Language and Liberty in Ghanaian Political Communication: A Critical Discourse Perspective', *Ghana Journal of Linguistics* 7(2): 199–224.

US Commission on Civil Rights Report. 2010. *Commission's Report of the March 12 Meeting*. Retrieved 16 July 2019 from https://www.usccr.gov/calendar/trnscrpt/031210ccr.pdf.

Chapter 1

'FOXES HAVE DENS BUT I AM HOMELESS'
On the Lived Experiences of a Homeless Man and His Social Worker

Hannah Kelling

This chapter is structurally organized into two parts: the lived experiences of a homeless person, Mark, and those of a caregiver who works with homeless people, respectively. In the first part, Mark, the homeless man, elucidates how he became homeless, the trials and tribulations associated with homelessness, and how he was fighting to survive despite life's strong currents flowing against his efforts. In the second part, Andrea, a caseworker with the Peace Shelter Center in Bloomington, Indiana, narrates her experiences in assisting the homeless. Andrea's qualities of sweetness and toughness as well as calmness and self-assurance amid cacophony and chaos are what make her perfectly suited for the position she holds.

Homelessness: The Sad But Inspiring Story of Mark

Introduction

When Mark and I sat down for our interview, we were very nearly strangers. A few short minutes before we opened the door to the small conference room, Andrea had provided us with a short introduction. Somewhat awkwardly, we marched our way up the stairs and away from the commotion of the hospitality desk. It had been a particularly busy morning of volunteering for me, with an unexpected wave of warm weather driving people inside to seek out short-sleeved T-shirts and deodorant. Even as we sat down to talk, I felt my mind still racing around between the various file cabinets and closets downstairs. I pondered: 'Did I put Mr. Jameson's mail folder back? Did they restock the hat drawer? Have they lost the Sharpie marker again?'

Mutual curiosity hung in the air as I shut the door to the tiny room where our interviews were to be conducted. The atmosphere changed slightly as Mark read over the Study Information Sheet that I had provided. In fact, he grew visibly agitated. When I asked why, he asked me what the title 'Co-Investigator' entailed. To the best of my ability, I explained that the term simply identified me as a researcher working on a university-approved research project. I assured him that I was not a law-enforcement officer, nor was I attempting to arrest him. The soothing effect that these words induced was minimal, although he did attempt to lighten the mood by asking what I studied. Altogether, it seemed that our interview was off to a rocky start.

As will be seen from this narrative, Mark's experiences with homelessness were convoluted and deeply personal. Although he barely knew my name, he seemed to feel quite comfortable sharing intimate anecdotes in response to my probing questions. Furthermore, he certainly did not shy away from bluntly reminding me of my good fortune and privilege. I found his frank way of communicating both refreshing and unsettling. He had spoken with a demeanour that had grown strangely familiar – sociable yet unapologetic, somewhat good-humoured, and yet sharply cynical. It was an uncanny mix that I had come to associate with the homeless archetype – a hardened vulnerability that seems impossible but that nevertheless exists in the words and the bearing of this roving population.

How Did It Happen?

Once we got past the initial awkwardness of the informed consent process, the interview gained a life of its own. Despite my attempts to be a neutral observer, I could not help but notice the unexpected freshness of Mark's appearance. He wore a clean T-shirt, boots with intact soles and faded jeans that nonetheless had a somewhat modern style. If I had passed him on the street, I might never have realized that he spent most nights up the road at the co-ed shelter. In fact, he spent his first night at the shelter in the autumn of 2016 – more than a year before the time of our interview. That is where our interview began:

HANNAH KELLING: *How long have you considered yourself homeless?*

MARK: Let's see . . . I guess, really, I've probably been homeless since sometime in 2016. Me and my son's mother, we lived up in Indianapolis. Whenever that all fell apart, we lived with her sister . . . When I look back on it, I knew that wasn't going to work out. Where were we going to go next? Obviously, we were going to have to go stay with somebody else. So, the last place I had with my name on a lease . . . It's been since 2016. Almost two years now.

The first time I stayed at [the shelter] was in October. I stayed one night, but I freaked out, had temporary psychosis (that's what they called it) and, when I got out of jail . . . I went back down South. But, then, I ended up coming back up that December and I stayed at [a different shelter] for . . . like two weeks, I think, maybe. I've left a couple of times. Sometimes I go down to Bedford to old friends' houses and just hang out. Couch surf.

[Prior to that] I had been bouncing around . . . 2015, it would have been . . . Well, and then before that I guess I was homeless, too.

HK: It's been a while.

M: Yeah, I'd say . . . Now that I'm thinking about it. I guess, honestly, I've had three stints. I'd say five years.

HK: Is it easy to point out one thing that happened?

M: Hmm . . . I mean, there's an accumulation of things. Like, now, I don't have a place to stay. When I went back down South to stay with some friends for a while, I got a job. So, I called my old landlord and she ended up giving me an apartment. But I didn't ever move in. I had to get an old electric bill paid off before she'd let me move in. Also, I was going to court for a protective order. I got granted five hours of visits with my child a week. And, I had to drive up here to pick him up. We had to go back down to Mitchell to church, and then we had to drive him all the way back up here. It was stressful to everyone.

So, a couple weeks later, I met up with my old sponsor and we were talking and hanging out. I'd been off drugs for almost two years at that point. I began drinking heavily, though. And the drinking is what led up to me and my kid's mom splitting up. At least, that's what she, ya know, . . . That was her 'reason'. I'll never figure that out.

My kid and his mom, they used to live right across the street from here (the shelter) in a white house. So, I thought I would see him all the time. I would be closer to him, I guess. That made me feel better about it. So, I went down to [my friend's house] that night and picked my clothes up and came back up here.

HK: So, all things considered, is there any one thing you could say led to your homelessness?

M: I'm homeless by choice. Originally, anyway, it was by choice. And that choice was because I wanted to be close to my kid.

At this point, my head was spinning. We were scarcely five minutes into the interview and Mark had already achieved an astonishing level of self-disclosure. His speech was rushed, as though the words had been waiting just below the surface for a long time, waiting for the opportunity to come out. In effect, he had a voice that hitherto had been muted by circumstances beyond his control. He only needed a listening ear and the interview provided an opportunity to verbalize his 'hidden' story.

As Mark continued to answer my first few questions, his Genesis story – the story of how and why he had become homeless – began to take shape. Repeatedly, he asserted that homelessness had originally been his choice. His rendition of the above assertion was delivered with an odd tone and demeanour, somehow a simultaneous mix of bashfulness and confidence. Was he being defensive? It was as though he recognized that choosing homelessness was irrational but claiming that he had done so was the only way to maintain some sense of agency regarding the course of his life. If he admitted that any factor other than himself had caused him to lose his home, he would have to relinquish control over his own narrative – a difficult psychological shift, one might say.

Consistent with this initial impression, two themes emerged. The first was the theory of *choice* and *family* – Mark had chosen homelessness to be present in his son's life. The second theory was darker in nature and centred on a common scapegoat of and for homelessness; *addiction*. I am no expert and can hardly diagnose this medical condition, but it seemed possible that based on inferences gathered from Mark's discursive renditions and his nonverbal cues, one could rightly speculate that his personal life choices and family commitments as well as addiction might have played a role in his becoming homeless. For now, we will return to the narrative where we left off:

HK: Do you see your son often, now?
M: I haven't seen my kid in a long [time] . . . Almost a year.
HK: Is that by choice?
M: Pfft! No. His mother's choice. Her choice. She put a protective order against me. She sorts of let me see him after I got my job back at the signage shop here in town. Then, in her true asshole nature . . . As soon as I got laid off: new protective order. She said I'm a 'piece of shit' and this, that, and the other thing. I went to rehab last year, and we went back to court because she got another protective order.

I've made some bad decisions in the past couple weeks. It's my kid's birthday on the 7th. I've been trying to get money together, so I could go see him. And, I don't even know where the f--- he's at. Well, he lives in Indianapolis now with his mother. They moved.

I became homeless for an admirable reason. . .
HK: But, with your family gone, why stay in Bloomington?

M: I have nowhere else to go. My family's in Mitchell and they don't speak to me. You know, I've been in and out of jail since I was eighteen. And, I would just stay away from [home] if I was out of jail because I was getting high. I've been a drug addict since I was fifteen, and if you're not doing the same thing that a drug addicts are doing, they're going to go to where people *are* doing what they're doing. I didn't want to sit at Thanksgiving dinner – even sober – and feel like I'm being looked at, or looked down upon, I guess. So, I'll go eat at the [*unintelligible*] rather than eating turkey with people who are judging me.

HK: So, that [*feeling of rejection*] *pushed you out of home?*

M: Yeah, but there are no homeless shelters in Morris County. No homeless shelter in Orange County. No homeless shelter in any county I know of down South. Maybe Evansville, once you get into those bigger towns. So, yeah, you got to go where there's shelter.

Later, when I asked Mark about his most pressing concerns, his answer was as follows:

M: Getting arrested on some kind of warrant for dealing. 'Cause if I have the opportunity to get something from someone . . . Or, if someone gave me something like cigarettes or something like that . . . and I have the opportunity to sell it, I'm going to. And that's just all there is to it. It's called surviving.

Mark's countenance became more and more troubled as we continued with this line of conversation. He claimed to have originally chosen homelessness for the sake of his family, but that same family had actively pushed him away. At least partly to blame for this separation were the haunting effects of addiction – something he alluded to throughout the interview but rarely talked about explicitly, perhaps out of shame, perhaps because he was nervous about my role as an 'investigator' or perhaps because he did not attribute much significance to it. Regardless, it became obvious that the addictive effect was too great for him to overcome and he no longer knew how to extract himself from the homeless life he had 'chosen'. He had 'stagnated' and he knew it. And from that stagnation rose a sense of both embarrassment and cynicism regarding the have/have-not structures of society.

Have/Have-Not

Despite our vastly different backgrounds, Mark and I were able to talk openly for most of the interview. However, there were moments when the 'rift' between us seemed to open up. In those moments, Mark would vent his frustrations regarding various public systems – law enforcement, housing, etc. – that seemed to serve and protect what he saw as a privileged class at the expense of people experiencing homelessness. One such dialogue began as presented below. We were talking about the local park and a recent effort by local law-enforcement and city officials to discourage homeless individuals from loitering there. Mark's frustration with the subject quickly became obvious:

HK: Did you have friends who lived in the park?

M: I mean . . . I knew some folks who would sleep there. But I don't know if I'd call it 'living' there. Nobody is living in the parks. Not in ------- Park or --------- Park. Even if they sleep there every night, it's not living there. It's just not!

HK: Did you talk with people about how [the new ordinance within the park] affected them?

M: Yeah, it affected the homeless community as a whole. Because, basically, the city ordered 'Marshal' law at [the park].

HK: I haven't heard it put that way before.

M: And that . . . That's a scary thought. I mean, nobody did anything about it. I remember the news people coming into town and shit and – I hate to say it – but you've got f---in' [the community centre director] deciding who – out of us – gets to talk to them next. It's just awkward, ya know? The guy that runs one of the only places where we can come and have even the basics, was deciding who's going to talk to the news. That's not a decision that he gets to make.

HK: You think that it should be. . .

M: But, if we were to make a stink about it, you'd be in fear that you'd be kicked out of here. And if you've already been kicked out Wheeler, then you can't go there for lunch or dinner, and then you can't come here for lunch or breakfast . . . Then, you're stuck with the community kitchen that's open one time a day.

It makes you wonder if the higher up's and the city and people that are helping in organizations around town – if they're not in cahoots also! Thinking to themselves: 'Let's keep the town looking better. No, we don't want to throw more money at housing. Screw that. Screw the people. Just keep them the f--- out of sight.'

HK: Well, you know that [two Housing First apartment complexes] went up recently? How do you feel about those projects?

M: I feel like it's f---ing bullshit that some of the ones that are in there are in there, and yet I scored three points too low to get into [those housing units] because I'm just not messed up enough. But my credit and financial history is so f---ed that I can't – I won't. . .

There's the [Housing First] programme, and then there is Rapid Rehousing. Well, last year I was in Rapid Rehousing. I had a good job and all that. I turned in the application to rent everywhere. I spent over $400 in applications and got denied by everyone. At that point everyone was just standing around looking at me like: 'What are we gonna do?'

Well, I don't f---ing know! That's what you're here for, ya know?

I timed out on the however-many-days you had to find a place, and just was in danger of getting kicked out of the shelter because I couldn't find a house to live in within their 45-day timeframe with my f---ing f---ed up credit. And, I told them all those things!

So, this year, I retook the test because I went down to Jasper for the summer. For about 2½–3 months I was down there, and it didn't work out. So, I came back up here to go to [a rehabilitation centre] and dry out. And, I turned myself in for a 'failure to appear' on my criminal case. So, when I came back up here, I had to take their evaluation again – or whatever – for housing. I went from like an 8 or a 9 to like 14 or 16. They said the highest score was like 16. Either way, I was just under. And, the woman who's in charge of Crawford; I was talking to her about when my name would be put on the list and she was like: 'You'll never get in. You don't score high enough', she said. 'And we always put the highest scoring people in first.'

Well, you could take [those high-scoring people] and they could stay at the shelter, since they're so in need of protection. It makes no sense to me why that person gets more attention.

HK: *So, if the city could do two things, or one thing . . . What do you think should be [the priority]? What could they do to better serve you?*

M: Well, the City owes me nothing! That's the thing! But, you know, if the City wanted to . . . There's obviously a problem for the City and the people who have money in this town. They don't like it – for people to go walk around in dirty clothes. But, if you have a problem with the problem, don't make a bigger problem out of it! Try to help fix it rather than just bitch at it. It doesn't make no sense to me.

The City wants us out of the parks because it looks bad. And, that's exactly what it is. It LOOKS bad. They're going to say: 'It's this' or 'It's that' or what the 'frick' ever. 'There are dirty needles everywhere' or 'There's drinking'. First of all – with drinking – there are college kids running up and down these streets downtown, drinking like a f---ing fish. Why is it different? Because they have money.

HK: *That's a big point.*

M: And if you don't like how it looks with needles everywhere . . . Well, put a f---ing disposal box.

HK: *Why do you think they don't do that?*

M: Have you seen this one back here? [*Gestures to behind the shelter building*] I mean, it looks ridiculous. But the fact of the matter is it's the world we live in today. I don't think more privileged people . . . I don't know, you seem prim and proper, like you probably come from a pretty decent family with a little bit of money. You would be, first off, 'culture shocked' to be thrown from that into this. But the world is changing into such a negative thing that, I don't know. . . I don't think anybody's really prepared for what's about to happen. When I say 'about' I don't mean there's going to be some sort of catastrophic event here soon and I know it. I haven't talked to some burning bush . . .

It's just that, by the end of it, like, what people have to do to survive is going to be just short of war. Like the shit we did in Vietnam to people, and what they did to our people. That's just going to be a normal everyday thing to get f---ing food. And, I mean, a lot of us already feel like we're fighting to survive. You've got the cops watching you all the time. . .

HK: *You mentioned Marshal law earlier.*

M: Yeah, I mean . . . I'll call it 'stalking'. It's profiling. 'We heard from this person. He's dealing drugs. We have no proof, but they said you were. Now, we have reason to follow you.'

Well, I also heard that Billy over there who graduated from IU; he's selling drugs, too! Or he's selling child porn, or he's doing whatever, but . . . they don't care. Billy's mommy and daddy donate to the school. Billy's mommy and daddy don't like that they have to look at homeless people when they want to go to [the bar] to get drunk with their son.

HK: *That's another big point!*

M: They moved everybody out of [the local park] due to money. They feel like there would be more money. I don't see how the frick anybody in this town could think there's MORE money because you move the homeless people. What are you gonna do? Build a bar? There are plenty of those.

You know, [the bar owner] is bitchin': 'We're losing business!' Bullshit. You ain't! I've been in there at 2:00 in the afternoon on a Tuesday and it's f---in' packed. Ya know? It's just . . . It's a culture thing, I guess, when it comes down to it. You watch TV and the news, and you know . . . And, you're taught that the homeless people are dirty and they're bad people and they did terrible things. That's what you're taught.

There were people who were allowed to speak to the media about the plight of the homeless in Bloomington – and then there was Mark. There were people who could access the Rapid Rehousing programmes – and then there was Mark. There were people who could afford to drunkenly wander the streets of town with no more than an eyeroll – and then there was Mark.

Mark's narrative is replete with examples of individuals who have what he does not. The frustration this causes was palpable. Despite his earlier attempts to take responsibility for his homelessness, Mark seemed to recognize that these constructs of privilege and positionality – systems that promote a dichotomy of 'Haves' and 'Have-Nots' – were at least partially to blame for his continued homelessness. What if he had scored just a few points higher on the housing scale? Would he have had an apartment? What if his parents had been able to afford his college education? Would he have been able to go out for a drink without being questioned by law enforcement?

These questions hung in the air like a stubborn sour smell as we continued our interview.

Failure

The third and last theme that emerged from our interview was a natural consequence of a have/have-not system: failure. As was mentioned in the preceding section, multiple public structures and authority figures had failed Mark throughout his life. His lingering feelings of disappointment will become even more obvious in this concluding section of his narrative. Unable to access appropriate services and forced to continually appeal to others for help, a corollary theme of shame also took a firm shape in life and hence his discourse.

First, we will examine these complex emotions within a thread of conversation described earlier in this narrative, one in which he outlined the difficulties that arose from his partner's protective order:

M: I was going to court. Somebody at the church I was attending down there brought me up there for that protective order. And that went horribly wrong. When I got granted visits with my child, my pastor did the same thing. I had a job [at that time], but I didn't have any money to give the guy.

HK: *To give the pastor for helping you?*

M: Yeah, for bringing me up there. So, a couple weeks later, he dropped me off for criminal court. A misdemeanour criminal trespassing. He had to go to work, though ... And when I got to thinking about it, I was feeling bad about all that shit – about having to drive back and forth and somebody else having to take care of me. They were, and they still are. And it, ahh ... [*Mark exhaled sharply*] So, I that screwed the apartment issue and all that.

We went back to court because she got another protective order. The judge did not even ask any questions for evidence. You know, nothing! Granted it for two years, and . . . All of it was a lie. Everything she put in there was a lie. And it was amazing to me, that the judge would just do that.

It messes me up. Those protective orders . . . They have to give your initial report to the judge. And the judge is supposed to read over it and decide whether it's enough evidence to, ya know, file. Or no, I'm sorry. They instantly file it. And then you go to court. And that's when the judge is supposed to ask questions and get to the bottom of it. And, that's fine.

But when the original reports go in . . . The judge signed it. You know, the same judge that sat there and made the final decision! She had her f---in' mind made up when she signed it the first time. So, now I'm trying to convince the powers that be to change their mind . . . And, it's a judge. Usually, their decision is their decision. They don't change their mind later on. That seems extremely unfair to me. And, I just don't understand where they get off doing that.

HK: *How much you think the powers that be – whether that's park managers in my field or judges or whoever – how much do they have your interests in mind?*

M: Oh, well, they all have our interests in mind! They're interested in what the f--- we're doing. They're not interested in helping.

It blows my mind when you get such a large amount of complaints that you tell people they cannot be in the public park or they're going to get arrested or be given trespassing charges or loitering tickets . . . Just because 90% of them are out there, f---ed up, doesn't mean that the other 5% are doing anything other than trying to survive. And they don't know what happens. They don't know why they're homeless, the police, the city . . . You know?

HK: *Were you in [the local park] during the shift?*

M: No. I would go down there once in a while to talk with people. But just standing around in the parks is not my thing. I can agree that it is – that it looked horrible down there. It looked like a shanty town. Without the little cardboard houses. But, still, that's their right as individuals! To be on public property. Free to do what they want. Within the law. No matter what, they're not trespassing unless they've been banned? And they can't ban someone from public property.

And, I'll be the first one to say: 'OK, I don't care if you're homeless or not. You do not have to look like that.' You know? That's laziness. And maybe mental things they've got going on . . . I understand that. I understand that all too well. But. . .

Mark's sense of disillusionment was apparent. In his eyes, the court system operated on a *guilty-until-proven-innocent* basis in which the judges had their minds made up long before the trial began. Public servants were not motivated to solve real problems – they were motivated to pry into the lives of those less fortunate. At the mercy of these unsympathetic forces, Mark seemed to have contracted this contagious and disapproving attitude towards people experiencing homelessness. He tried to set himself apart from those squatting in the public parks in their 'shanty town'. At one point during our interview, he even blurted out: 'I feel like I'm probably smarter than 95% of the people who are homeless here.'

From Mark's narrative, we begin to understand the frustration one must feel as the member of a mercilessly stigmatized group. It would also seem that Mark, to relieve some of that cognitive discomfort, sought to elevate himself in comparison to the 'typical' person experiencing homelessness. Whether these efforts were successful in relieving his pain remains open for debate.

To end our interview, I wanted to capture the rhythm of Mark's life in a description of his day. I thought that this would be a relatively light-hearted subject of conversation and a comfortable decrescendo from our other, more agitating topics. I was wrong, as can be seen in our interaction below:

HK: Can you walk me through a typical day? If there is such a thing?

M: Well, these last couple of days haven't been typical . . . But, a typical day . . . I'll just go through what a typical day used to look like: I'd get up at the shelter anywhere between 4:30 and 7:00 AM, you know. Just depends on what time I got up. I would just drink coffee and go outside and smoke a cigarette and get ready for the day. Sit and watch the news – they [the shelter staff] turn the TV on for a little bit. And then I had to leave the shelter by quarter-till 8:00. I'd come down here . . . Which is another thing: These places run that place. They're 'affiliated' – doesn't matter how they word it. When it's 30°F outside, why is this place not open before that place closes?

HK: You mean, to prevent [an uncovered gap] in time. . .

M: Yeah, I don't understand that. People always act like they want to make sure that we know . . . That they feel the power. I'm not really sure how that goes.

HK: So, when those places close, there's a little lag. . .

M: Yeah, this place used to not open until 8:15. So, we'd stand out there in that parking lot for a half hour. And we just froze. I mean, it's absolutely freezing. And the f---ed up part? At that point, there would be three to four [staff members] just standing there. It's just kind a . . . kind a crazy.

HK: And when these doors open up. . .

M: I'd eat breakfast here. And I would leave from here at 9:00 AM and walk to the library because the library opens at 9:00 AM. I'd hang at the library until noon, watch movies online. And then . . . [*pause*] Or work, you know. At one point, I had a job. I worked 10 hours a day and I worked four days a week.

HK: What job was that?

M: [A signage shop on the west side of town.]

But, yeah . . . I'd watch movies, surf the web, whatever. Sit in this little area where you could talk and, you know, bullshit with other homeless people. Come down here [to the shelter] and eat lunch, go back to the library. . .

Here, Mark laughed bitterly, as though disgusted by the slow routine of his day:

HK: And in the evening?

M: I'd go back to the shelter and watch TV.

With this being a 'Housing First' place, they say their main concern is to get you housed . . . Bullshit. Their main concern is to get more funding. So, they won't house the people that they should. Because they know that they'll get kicked out. But it doesn't matter that they get kicked out in 30 days because they got them housed.

We can turn in our paperwork every f---in' time – every 30 days to the same apartment. It doesn't matter if there are twelve people in that apartment that year. They housed twelve people.

HK: I'll admit – I don't know how that system works.

M: I don't think anybody could sit down and tell you consistently how it works because there is no consistency. And I know that there's no consistency in the world . . . I understand that. It's just that when people lie . . . Just be honest about it.

HK: About what you can and can't do.

M: Yeah! I just want honesty. So, housing is a big concern. And I guess, work [would be another top concern]. Getting a job. Any job, I want it. Any job. Like, if you asked me: 'Do you want [the shelter director]'s job?' Doesn't matter if I've never had a job like that before, I would do it better than [he] does it. I fully think that in my mind. Maybe I wouldn't, but . . . I mean, I'm just not mentally stable enough right now, I guess.

HK: Which is part of why housing is a big concern, maybe? To help you stabilize a little.

M: Yeah, yeah . . . My own space. Just somewhere where I know what's what.

Everyone wants their own house so that they can do whatever they want. I guess they forget you can do whatever you want regardless of where you're at. It's the consequences; that's the real reason. Because they don't want to face consequences for what they do.

With the above rendition, our 45-minute interview ended. Rather abruptly, Mark stood up from his chair and moved towards the door, talking about a warrant under his breath. I did my best to reassure him, repeating the fact that I was no more than a researcher and thanking him for his time. He seemed soothed, but only slightly. In a moment, we parted ways and I would not see him again during my time as a volunteer. I will expand on this in the final section of this chapter.

Caring for the Homeless at the Peace Shelter

Andrea, the interviewee in this section, had one of those rare countenances that manages to exude sweetness and toughness simultaneously. Her smile is gracious, welcoming and a little playful. But her squared shoulders and the confident way she meets your gaze serve as a reminder that she is no stranger to confrontation. As she makes her way through the tight hallways of the Community Shelter, she navigates a myriad of new faces and intermittent requests with an unhurried manner. It was simply another day for Andrea, who had been a caseworker with the Community Shelter where she worked for almost two years at the time of this interview. A small, slightly dishevelled desk on the ground floor constitutes her personal territory in this old building. Tucked in a room separated from the hospitality area by a couple of thin partitions, it is there that she conducts her daily round of meetings with members of the community's homeless population.

When I joined the fluid team of volunteers for a regular Thursday morning shift almost four months ago, I remember hearing Andrea laugh from around the corner. As I scrambled to collect an armful of mini shampoo bottles, chapstick and other toiletries for the most recent guest at the counter, I found myself wondering how a person could sound so calm and self-assured in the middle of so much chaos. Later in my tenure as a volunteer, I remember when one of our guests began vocalizing unsolicited compliments to the female staff, most of which were shrugged aside or accepted with red-faced embarrassment, but not by Andrea! She took one kind, yet stern look at our young guest and said: 'I know I look good, but I don't want to talk about that at work, thanks!' Thinking back, I feel another wave of admiration for that tactful, no-nonsense way of making one's preferences known. It is simply Andrea's way.

When I contacted the Director for Center Programming at the community centre about interviewing one of their caseworkers, Andrea's name was proffered almost immediately. She was eager to participate and was excited to connect me with one of her clients when the time came to interview a chronically homeless individual.

Despite being put in the hot seat, Andrea was undoubtedly the more poised individual during our interview, which lasted for nearly an hour. We fell into an easy conversational rhythm, and I had to consistently remind myself to take a step back into my neutral researcher stance. When I did so, I began to understand that Andrea's vivacious and friendly mien was a fundamental part of an impenetrable professional façade. As we began to speak pointedly about her motivations for pursuing a career in casework and her own personal theories about why homelessness exists, it took some prodding for us to move from the broad brushstrokes of 'How?' and 'Why?' into more personal anecdotes. Whether this was due to my relative inexperience as a qualitative interviewer or Andrea's resistance to intimate disclosures, it is hard to say. However, by the time we parted ways, a few personal tales had bubbled to the surface, which provided some insight into the lived experience of a caseworker working with the homeless population.

Being 'in It'

No desk is occupied by accident. Once upon a time, Andrea took her first steps out into the adult world and a nearly endless array of occupational options lay within reach. Among the many choices, Andrea had opted for the close halls of this bustling community centre, and I could not help but wonder how and why she had done so. Our discourse interaction, given below, explicates the above assertion and leads us into another aspect of Andrea's lived experience:

HANNAH KELLING: *Why did you choose to become a caseworker and – specifically – did you make a conscious choice to work with this population at this point in your life? Let's go down memory and motivation lane for you.*

ANDREA: Yeah! So, when I first started working here, I had worked for an agency for about seven years that assisted people with disabilities. I was managing group homes and I was working with clients who had pretty severe behavioural issues. They were pretty physically aggressive. I was working like 70–80 hours a week doing that, and I was trying to get back into school [full-time] because going to school and working that many hours wasn't working out. So, I knew that I was going to have to make a change. My roommate at the time was already working here and she was transitioning from her position as an Outreach worker to the Program Director of Friend's Place. I knew about what she was doing as an Outreach worker and thought it was really interesting! Sure, there were some things about it that made me really nervous. Like, you're going into the woods and looking for people, and you're by yourself! But I reminded myself that I had been getting beat up by these grown men for the last couple years. So, I thought I could handle this.

So, I had originally applied for that [Outreach] position because I wanted to be OUT and IN IT, you know? In return, I was offered another position here in the Rapid Rehousing programme. I took it. Once again, it was super interesting. This population is really interesting in general. Also, I just needed a new job! [*Laughter.*]

So, I worked with the Rapid Rehousing unit for a little over a year before transitioning downstairs where I felt like I was 'in it' a little bit more.

HK: *So, how do you feel about your current spot?*

A: Very good. So, with Rapid Rehousing, I was working up here [referring to the upstairs part of the community centre building, where the administrative offices are located]. In this unit, you are very disconnected to what's going on downstairs. There, you know who people are. Here, you don't. People were being referred to me who were living outside and experiencing all these things, but I didn't feel like I had a really true idea of what those things were. In broad terms, I understood it, but I didn't actually know *what that's like* for you. Of course, when they come to us [the administrative personnel, specifically those in Rapid Rehousing programmes], hopefully they're just homeless a couple more weeks. Then, we get them housed! That was wonderful; it was so wonderful to be able to give someone the keys to their apartment. Like, 'Here ya go! Here's your place! By the way, we're going to pay for it for a minute!' But I think that being downstairs is a better fit for me. I get really chatty, and I like all the new faces and getting to talk to all the people. So, even on those days when we're super busy and we've already seen twenty people before noon . . . I feel like I kind of thrive off of that, you know. That fast pace, and just getting it done. Downstairs, I'm 'in it'.

As our interview began to gain momentum, it became clear that Andrea preferred to avoid a 'sidelined' role. While it was certainly rewarding to hand over the keys to an apartment at the end of a person's arduous journey with homelessness, Andrea felt that when upstairs, she had often missed the opportunity to engage with the homeless at their most vulnerable state. Therefore, four months before our interview, she had requested a transfer from the upstairs Rapid Rehousing programme office to the downstairs Caseworker cubicle. From that vantage point, the workday operated a little differently. Andrea was no longer a vague presence in the final stage of the process; she was a major part of the lives of the homeless. She was 'in it':

HK: So, could you describe a 'typical day' in the life of caseworker Andrea?

A: Yeah! So, on typical day, I normally roll out of bed about 20 minutes before I'm supposed to be here. I live down the street, so it's really convenient. I come in, and I usually come in through the back door, so I can walk through the kitchen and catch people while they're in the breakfast line. That's kind of nice sometimes because I can get an eye on who's already here. If there's anybody that I need to talk to that day, I can snag them while they're waiting for breakfast and say: 'Hey, eat your food and then come see me.' I try to get my hooks in them early.

HK: Just try to facilitate that meeting, huh?

A: Right, yeah! Then I usually swing by Sharon's desk and I check in with her, kind of let her know what I'm doing that day. And, also, I just chat with her sometimes. You know, work . . . Then I head back to my desk and we check messages. We have like five or six phones that we have to check every day.

HK: How many messages pile up on there?

A: There was one day where there were fifty! But, usually, between all of the lines, we might get about twenty messages. But a lot of those will be hang-ups or automated messages where somebody is using this as their phone number and some company or debt collector is calling. Somebody who is not actually leaving information, and we don't have a name.

So, we start by just deleting all of that, and then we filter through the rest. Around 9 AM, we start seeing people. Hopefully, it's exactly at 9 AM . . . But sometimes it goes over a little bit, depending on what needs to be done. Or, sometimes somebody is having an emergency and I have to bring them back right away before 9 AM. Which, then, kind of pushes my morning back, and then I'm trying to catch up on emails throughout the day. It depends on that first hour. And then, you know, we just start pulling people off the list.

Yesterday, our list had filled up and we had seen all 20 people before 12 PM! There are some days when people just need small things. [Yesterday], we were with each person for maybe 10 minutes. So, yeah, there are some days when you just have these little things and sometimes things take longer. You might have to call and help with insurance, and then you're sitting on hold for 30 minutes. [The specific need] can really determine how quickly we're able to move through the list. Our goal is to see twenty people and on a standard day, and that's usually about right.

HK: *What would you say is the most people you could see in a day? Or the most you've seen?*

A: Yesterday . . . If the clients were going like they were, and the meetings were quick (10–15 minutes), we probably could see like forty people.

HK: *Oh my gosh. In just one day . . . And I know you guys have about 140 for breakfast in the morning?*

A: Yeah, lots of people. And there's a large portion of people that come in frequently, so I have about fifteen to twenty people that I see on a regular basis. And then, you know, maybe another 25–50% during the week that are just new faces. Those people may be housed, but they're coming in here to get financial assistance for something or because they have a question. Or they might be people who are new to the area or newly homeless and have found their way in here. Really, it can be a little bit overwhelming sometimes because there's just a lot of new faces and new people to try to keep track of.

As Andrea spoke, the muffled sounds of many indistinct voices could be heard through the floor of the tiny conference room. The brief description provided above is a humble summary of what can be a demanding job, especially when poor weather or a rowdy guest creates an unusual stir.

The interview progressed and we eventually moved from a description of how Andrea found her way into the fray to a moment of musing about the importance of empathy. This portion of the interview had to be carefully administered because I was aware of how too little effort on my part could lead to failure to connect with Andrea (or any interviewee for that matter), while being overly 'zealous' could lead to my unravelling.

Baggage and Backstory

As she described the volume of people who appear at her desk in a typical day, Andrea voiced an important point:

A: When you sit down with somebody, you always have to remember to ask them: 'Who are you? Where did you come from, specifically? What was your story before this?' Sometimes, depending on the day, it's hard to get all of that information. But then you notice later that this person seems like they're really vulnerable and it's like: 'Oh, sh--! I should have gotten all of that important stuff.'

HK: *All the baggage and backstory.*

A: Yeah. . .

HK: *How well do you think you understand what life is like outside of Peace-Place Living on the street?*

A: I think that I understand it a little bit more. I thought that I knew less than I did when I was upstairs because I just *felt* that disconnect. There were some things where I felt like: 'OK . . . I think I've got this idea.' And I know that it's still not to the point of the Outreach work, where you're actually *there* and seeing it . . . But I think that I'm getting to see people's day-to-day struggles more, like small insurance things and how much things can affect them while they're still outside and not within shelters. Trying to help people access those really basic services has definitely given me a wider breadth of knowledge – an understanding of the real nitty-gritty issues of our clientele.

At this point, we had examined homelessness through the professional lens of caseworker Andrea. But we were at least 20 minutes into our interview before the personal relevance of this vulnerable population became evident. In response to an unrelated question where I asked Andrea to speculate about the causes of homelessness, she delivered a stirring personal anecdote about her own family member's brush with addiction and housing uncertainty. For a moment, the bubbly professional façade dropped, and the story unravelled one line at a time. Her countenance was serious, and her words were delivered first with a stumbling rhythm and then in a rush. The interview proceeded as follows:

HK: What do you then, see as the causes of homelessness?
A: I think that (for me) it's . . . So, I, one of my siblings . . . struggled with opiate addiction for about ten years. And, um, although he never became street-homeless, he was definitely homeless for about a year in the middle of his addiction. Our family didn't know where he was . . . He was bouncing around, you know . . . And so . . . I think about him, and how he had his family. Like, as his sister, I had to really draw those firm boundaries because it was screwing my life up. You know, [I got] to the point where I wasn't functioning in my day-to-day life because I was always worrying about him. 'Where is he? What's happening? Is he still alive?' That kind of stuff.
 I think for him, at that point in time, he was probably in a spot where it didn't seem like he had a support network. So, I guess I relate that to a lot of our clients. Like, these things happen and people just, you know, have to make whatever decision is going to best support them.
HK: So, having been there, you can kind of empathize with that [family/support network] role. There is only so much support you can provide before you have to take care of your own life.
A: Yeah, and . . . especially when substance abuse [is involved], and you feel like you could change it. If they would just get clean or make

that decision! I think that that's something the general community doesn't understand. It's not always that easy, making that decision to get clean. If you have a physical addiction to something, your body is the thing that is driving your life force at the moment.

HK: *So, I wanted to ask you specifically about what barriers you think clients experience in either getting care or connecting with services. These challenges can fall within a couple of different categories, like the caseworker–client relationship. Do you think there are barriers to getting services or interpreting each other the right way?*

A: Yeah, so I think as far as the caseworker–client relationship [is concerned] . . . I think that we're in a good position. For the most part, people are pretty honest with us when they come. I definitely have people just straight-up lie to me about their situation. But, generally, people are forthcoming. Or, they try to be.

Sometimes – in the instance of them not being super forthcoming with me – maybe it's pride. Maybe they could very well be in denial about how severe their situation is. You know, they might not trust me well enough – yet – to really let me in and let me know what's going on. Or, if they do, sometimes it happens that I just don't know where to refer them at the moment. Or, even if I do, those places may not be available. So, like with addictions issues, if we're trying to get them into a treatment centre it's like: 'Yeah, we can do that for you, but it might be a week before they can get you in', because they usually want them to detox before they go to the centre. So, trying to help a person, and then saying: 'You're going to have to detox outside . . . You know, you're definitely going to feel like you're dying, but please don't do those drugs.'

HK: *Even though you're on the street. . .*

[*Both laugh bitterly/uncomfortably.*]

A: Yeah, so, that's usually it . . . The fear. People are pretty afraid of [detoxing]. And, sometimes it's just an issue if we just can't get them to the services in a timely enough manner for them to be able to utilize them.

An uncomfortable pause filled the room for a moment as we both considered the incomprehensible pain of being forced to 'detoxify' on the street, fully exposed to the elements and the curious scornful gaze of strangers. Andrea's face was introspective and displayed a tinge of discomfort as though the hurt of an imagined addict was her own. The following dialogue therefore came as no surprise:

HK: *What personal characteristics do you think make you most capable or qualified for your position?*

A: So, I think I touched on that a little bit earlier: I'm kind of chatty and just like talking to people. And, I feel like I'm a personable person, so I definitely think that goes along with it. I can sit down with somebody and just kind of dig in with: 'Hey, how you doing? What can I help you with today?'

I used to always describe myself as being really empathetic. Then, I had a conversation with Kelly once where we were talking about empathy, and [we talked about] how it's actually empathy which burns out social workers and case managers. Because you're taking in that trauma. So, I have really tried to focus this last year on being more like sympathetic to people's situations. Like saying: 'Oh, I'm really sorry. That's a really terrible thing.' But generally maintaining a really firm boundary for myself. 'Your problem is not my problem.' Which sounds real crappy . . . And, I'm going to do what I can to help you solve that problem. Still, at the end of the day, I'm leaving at 4 PM, and I'm going to do my hardest to have that not be my problem.

I'm just trying to maintain that boundary. I think that it serves me, and it serves my clients in the long run because I can come into work every day and feel refreshed (or mostly. . .). Then, every once in a while, you get one that sneaks home with you.

HK: *Could you describe one that really stuck with you? One you did 'bring home'?*

A: Um, yeah . . . So, it's hard. Because there are different things. Things that have to do with young children; those can kind of stick with me because, oh, those *babies*! And to see them in such a bad situation. . . One that stuck with me . . . It was just because it was sad. It was actually a gentleman who had health insurance. And, I made the payment towards his premium because we were calling his health insurance to sort it out and he was just on [the basic plan]. So, I was like: 'Hey, I'm just going to make this payment for you.' And then he realized what was happening and he started crying . . . He was saying, 'I'm going to be able to go get glasses!'

I think with a lot of the men that come through here, they have had very hard lives. And they're very hardened. And, you know, they don't always show a lot of emotion and can be very gruff to deal with it. So, to have this man sitting there crying at my desk because he's going to be able to go get glasses? That one really, you know . . . I definitely went home that night and, as I was eating dinner and for the whole night, I just wanted to cry for this man. It seems like such a small, insignificant thing . . . 'Oh yeah, you can go get glasses now!'

The fact that he's been living this long not being able to do that . . . You know? So that was one that really like . . . Uhh! It *got* me!

HK: *Kind of unexpected, too, because it's 'just' glasses.*

A: Yeah, so that was one where I was just like: 'Ugh, this *hurt*. I need some ice cream!'

We both let out an easy laugh that faded into a hum of appreciation – how could such a simple thing be so pivotal? And how could one arrive at work each day energized and ready to face the full spectra of the human experience – paradoxical moments both achingly sweet and achingly sad? As I have demonstrated with the excerpts above, the balance of empathy and appropriate barriers constituted an important theme throughout our conversations. As Andrea mentioned, this balance served both herself and her clients in the end. She was able to speak from personal experience and connect on an intimate level with her clients, but she knew to draw back when she felt at danger of burning out. And, of course, there was always a tub of ice cream in the fridge for those especially challenging days.

Health Insurance: A Turning Point

Navigating the healthcare landscape is a complex task in the twenty-first century. Even for those whose healthcare plan is partially determined and sponsored by their employer, the array of choices can be overwhelming. What combination of premiums and deductibles is right for me? What services are covered and to what degree? What do I do if I cannot afford my co-payments? These questions are difficult to answer, and clarity can be near-impossible to achieve without proper internet access and financial advice. Early on in our interview, Andrea noted the pivotal role that health insurance can play in the progression of a homeless individual's life. For some, exorbitant medical bills contributed to their initial instability; for others, persistent health problems have deteriorated and remained largely unchecked because medical care is simply not affordable. It comes as no surprise, then, that Andrea's response to a question about the most important services involved health insurance and housing. The conversation proceeded as follows:

HK: What do you think are the three most important services that you provide?
A: I think probably one of the biggest ones is helping people get linked up with their health insurance. A surprising amount of people come through who just don't have insurance. And, to me, it feels like a relatively easy thing to get. So, that's one of the things that we try to get right away. It's one of the first questions that we ask because that can affect somebody's life so drastically!
If they get sick and lose their job, then they're not going to be able to maintain their housing or anything else in their lives. If you get sick or if

you get hurt, having that ability to go to the doctor and to get the care that you need is so vital. Nobody should end up with hundreds of thousands of dollars in debt because they have appendicitis. Many seem to have this option: 'I can die, or I can end up with a $60,000 hospital bill that I'm never going to be able to pay. And then that's going to destroy my credit. And nobody is going to want to rent to me because I'll have a super low credit score.'

You know, one of the things you see a lot is people who spend four days in the hospital and then they're released but they don't have anywhere to be released to. One person who I worked with last year had brain surgery and was released back into homelessness. And we ask: 'What do you do? How do you continue aftercare?' Having that health insurance piece is just so vital. Because that guy had complications and he already owed his doctor money. The likelihood that he was going to keep getting the care that he needs was pretty low.

HK: *And, if you add even one small problem to that situation, then you have a crisis.*

A: Yeah. So, I feel like I've had the biggest reactions from the clients when we're able to pay the premiums. For most of our clients, they don't have income, but they're required to pay $1 a month [to maintain insurance coverage]. So, we'll pay about $12 for the whole year. That will bump them up to [the more holistic plan]. Now, they don't have co-pays and they have prescription benefits. They can go see an optometrist or the dentist. Now, they have those really basic components of care.

We have so many clients with mental health issues or substance abuse issues and [with those ailments] you're not going to be able to get into any [shelter] – not ever. Some facilities – like Fairbanks – and like other places around the state require that you have health insurance. Some places offer scholarships, but then you're waiting even longer [to get in].

HK: *I talk with people about this sometimes – about how basic it is to see or to have feet that you can walk on all day. I take that for granted.*

A: Yeah, it's so amazing. That's actually one of the great things about the Peace-Place specifically. There are so many outside agencies and volunteers who come in and [meet those needs]. For the homeless to be able to access services here and not have to run around or spend half a day trying to find this location . . . It can be totally life-changing for them.

Earlier that day, two female volunteers had provided a free foot clinic for the guests of the community centre. Throughout the morning, they toiled over the blisters and callouses of the homeless. Overgrown nails were clipped, and tender spots were soothed. Feet that had carried weary souls for many cold months were finally given a brief respite. The foot clinic was one of few opportunities for the homeless to access healthcare services, and the packed sign-up list was evidence of an otherwise unmet need.

As I walked out of the shelter that day, my understanding of the pivotal role that healthcare can play in one's life was far deeper. And with each step, I felt a little more grateful for the condition of the feet that carried me.

The Big Picture: Why?

After discussing the pivotal role of health insurance, my curiosity was piqued. Steep medical bills may contribute to housing instability, but what did Andrea believe was the root cause of homelessness? Given her experience, could she identify one reliable answer? Or did she believe multiple factors were involved?

> HK: *Do you have a personal theory about why people are homeless?*
>
> A: I think one of the common things that I see throughout a lot of our clientele is a lack of support systems. If you have a friend or a family member that you could be staying with ... You would obviously be staying with them. Of course, sometimes, there are those secondary factors. Maybe there are some mental health or substance abuse issues – so, they're not able to stay with those people. Or, maybe, they just never had them to begin with. I feel like that's the root of it: there wasn't anybody around them who was willing or vaguely even capable of helping them dig themselves out of that hole. And, if you don't have that, then what do you do?
>
> Really, though, if you're experiencing the level of poverty that our clients face, you don't have access to healthcare. You may not even know the steps that you would take to go and find a doctor to start treating your mental illness. All of that comes from that support system.
>
> Some of these folks actually came from really good families! But, sometimes, you know, you just burn bridges and it's not necessarily anyone's fault. It just is the way it is. Interestingly, a lot of people come through who have master's degrees.
>
> HK: *That is especially notable for you – as someone going for a master's!*
>
> A: Yeah, that was definitely something that I wasn't expecting coming into this. People are homeless for all kinds of reasons and they come from all walks of life! But, then, there was one gentleman I was working with who used to be a math[s] professor ... and he's experiencing homelessness now. And, I wonder: 'How did this happen?' [They] went through a lot of school and that speaks to a level of organization that this person had in their life at one point in time. I want to ask: 'How did you lose the structure of your life?'

Personally, I can't make a huge generality ... But I think it's usually a drug issue that ends up coming into play. Then again – what if somebody just got bed bugs? If they [couldn't afford the chemical treatment], maybe they got evicted. Sometimes people just have really bad luck!

HK: *That's an interesting point! So, how accurate is the general population's perception of why people are homeless?*

A: Not very. They just see a lot of mental health issues. But [mental health issues] are not uncommon in the human population. Still, especially with substance abuse where it's one that you feel like you could change, people think: 'If they would just get clean or make that decision!' I think that that's something that the general community doesn't understand. It's not always that easy, making that decision to get clean. If you have a physical addiction to something, your body is the thing that is driving your life force at the moment.

HK: *What do you think of the community's attempts to mitigate the issue? Do you think there have been improvements?*

A: It can be hard to say. Within my immediate community, everybody's great! Everybody understands that addiction is more than a surface issue.

HK: *They think it's not just a vice. Like, there's more going on there.*

A: Yes. I think that the Indiana Alliance has had a really big impact with the new needle exchange programme. And, I know they have done a lot of work with the police. People aren't just going to be arrested for having syringes on them. It is illegal to have a syringe if you don't have a prescription for it ... But it's important that those people aren't being prosecuted because that's going to be a barrier for them in exchanging for and using clean needles.

HK: *Right. So, the word 'gentrification' has been associated with the redevelopment of [community's public park]. How do you feel about that situation? And has it changed the situation of the homeless as far as their needs, where they have to go?*

A: Hmm. When that was happening, I was still upstairs in Rapid Rehousing. So, a lot of the people that I was working with were not directly affected by it. But I remember going downtown and seeing people just camped out on the sidewalks with sleeping bags and all of their belongings.

I think that definitely – as a society – most people don't like to be confronted with the issue that there are really impoverished people out there. So, I think that it seemed probably like a good idea to just say: 'Just get them out of the park so we don't have to look at them.' But that doesn't mean that those people aren't still there.

But, of the people who are downtown at the parks, there is a pretty large percentage who aren't really homeless. They're just really poor. And the apartments are going up everywhere . . . They're not affordable, at least not for anybody who is making minimum wage.

So, I think that it has definitely become more of an issue. But, it's not necessarily a new one.

HK: *Thanks for that perspective. So, would you have any advice to a park professional or city council member working with this issue? What's the solution there?*

A: Just . . . Please don't call the police. I have so many clients who have these trespass orders. And as I'm looking through the cases, it seems that some people would have absolutely no criminal history at all if it weren't for these trespassing charges or charges for starting a fire in a public place (building a campfire or something like that). It's those problems which I just refer to as 'homeless problems'. They got arrested for homeless stuff. Because, you know, he was sleeping somewhere where he wasn't supposed to be.

I also understand the other side of that issue: to some people, that person is like a safety issue. Especially in parks when you have kids . . . I'm not blind to why they don't want people sleeping in the parks. But I would suggest getting in contact with your local service agencies like the Peace-Place or On-Board. We have outreach workers who can go out and find those people, engage with them and assess the situation. 'Why is this person here? What can we do to get them out of this spot?'

Lessons Learned

Mark's words left an indelible impact upon my mind, both as a researcher and as a fellow human being. I was struck by the shame and acridity that accompanied the begrudging description of his listless afternoons. Surely programmes exist that could provide him with a more productive use for his time — what some might call a purpose. Furthermore, one wonders whether there was some truth in the idea that simply living with a roof and four walls separating our daily lives from the natural world could somehow protect us from the consequences of our actions. These and a myriad of other thoughts and questions can be gleaned from Mark's narrative; it is important, not just for the reader but also for society at large, to ponder them and consider creative solutions that might benefit even the most resource-poor among us.

We learn from Andrea that medical bills, broken support networks and arrests accounted for some of the most common problems for the homeless. Andrea attributes the homelessness crisis to each of these issues and, likely, to a myriad of other factors that have appeared on a case-by-case basis. As can be seen from my interview with Mark, an element of choice may weave its way into some tales of homelessness as well.

There is no doubt that my own presuppositions, even prejudgements, about social work and homelessness may have played a role in my perception and interpretation of this interview data, and hence my subsequent identification of the overarching themes. Arguably, any trained (and sometimes even untrained) researcher has an unconscious influence upon the interviewed participant and the subject matter, making true objectivity impossible. Despite this, I found my conversation with Mark and Andrea to be enriching. Their interviews have provided considerable insights into the importance of homelessness in general and of being fully engaged with a homeless client in particular. Both narrators have also helped us gain insights into the need to carefully allocate sympathy, empathy and protective emotional barriers, and of helping with the navigation of the confusing network of essential healthcare services. These, and many others, appear to be the major themes of a homeless man and a caseworker's invisible stories. These stories thus serve as humble lessons for one and all.

Hannah Kelling grew up in the two-traffic-light town of Morrow, Ohio, as one of three triplets on a fifty-six-acre paradise. She holds a B.Sc. in Psychology from Kent State University and a M.Sc. in Recreation Administration from Indiana University-Bloomington, graduating *summa cum laude* from both institutions. She is a proud member of the Association for Experiential Education's leadership council in the Heartland Region and has worked in the outdoor recreation industry since 2013, first as a zipline tour guide and camp counsellor, and more recently as the coordinator of a trip and travel programme at an outfitter in Northeast Ohio. When she is not working, she enjoys guiding coastal kayaking tours with a local company, riding long distances on her hand-me-down bike and playing at open-mic nights with her partner.

Chapter 2

LIVING WITH ATAXIA
Nancy's and Lisa's Perspectives

Cassie Kresnye

This chapter involves two narratives that present the lived experiences of Nancy and Lisa, both living with ataxia, a condition associated with poor harmonization and shakiness of the body brought about by the brain's failure to control a patient's posture and normalize the strength and direction of their limb movements. Nancy's narrative is about the causes and devastating effects of ataxia on her balance and how she walks. She talks about her usual falls, her inability to walk straight, the various physical and neurological activities in which she is engaging, and her participation in drug and treatment trials and studies aimed at helping her to get well. She also narrates stories about support groups in which she has had to participate in order to stay healthy, as well as episodes of bravery and how she and her family have managed the disease.

In the second narrative, Lisa, a woman in her fifties, narrates, elucidates, and amplifies her lived experience with ataxia. She discusses the various tests and steps of going through neurologists and physicians of different specialities before being told she had ataxia. She commends her caregivers, who, she said, always stood by her, helped her, and encouraged her. She also narrates her stints with support groups and how they helped her to deal with her disease. Both Nancy's and Lisa's stories show how willpower and hope have helped them cope with their special health condition.

Nancy's Narrative

> My first look at ataxia was through the lenses of my mother.
> I see no magic pill or a magic treatment; I kind of have to retrain my brain, my cerebellum...
> —Nancy (interviewee), March 2018

Background

Settling down into my faded green secretary desk, I gently placed my interview question sheet on the cluttered workspace. This special day presented me with an opportunity to talk with an incredible person whom I had given the pseudonym Nancy. My heart raced with excitement as I glanced over my research questions placed on the small table by my side. I wondered what personal anecdotes, tales and/or narratives would be uncovered from my interaction with Nancy. The reminder I had set on my mobile phone clock for 4 o'clock PM rung out to my quiet room and I took a deep breath. I dialled the number and heard the first ring. The second ring echoed in my ear and I picked up my pen for notes. I had a few snippets written about Nancy and the journey she had experienced. Living in Indiana, Nancy had overcome many milestones in her life. Her encounter and subsequent 'relationship' with ataxia, a neurological disorder that affects a person's coordination and movement, began long before her own symptoms of the disease appeared, starting with her mother exhibiting symptoms of ataxia. Because of her lived experience with her mother's ailment, Nancy started her own ataxia journey with the wisdom and experience of what her mother went through. She was so much more than her disease and its diagnosis. She was a strong believer of the importance of education and, even with the medical issues she faced, she still tutored students once a week at a local school, helping them to learn to read. With the support of her loving husband and children, she continued to fight and overcome hurdles put in her way by the disease and all that came with it.

The third ring was cut off as a confident, but gentle voice answered on the other line. My pulse raced in my ears as I introduced myself. Nancy warmly responded; I could almost hear a smile on her face as we began to talk. With this, the interview proceeded as follows:

CASSIE KRESNYE: *What is ataxia to you?*
NANCY: Ataxia is different for each person, it's unique. For me, it affects my balance and the way I walk. I walk as if my legs are very heavy so it's kind of a gaudy kind of walk, and it's a walk that's similar to the way somebody who is intoxicated walks because it is very difficult to move

straight. That's something that is shared by everyone a little [*laughs*], I don't think anyone necessarily walks really straight, but I sway from side to side and it can be unpredictable.

CK: *Does ataxia affect other aspect of your coordination?*

N: Yes, I fall a lot. These aren't necessarily falls that I can explain why they happen; it's really just that my body can't control it [the disease or the fall]. These past couple of years, I've noticed my coordination going and especially how my walking is slowing, more than it previously was. Again, it's just difficult for me to sort of make my feet move faster and so I guess if somebody wants to know how far I can walk, I can probably walk about a mile and then my tired feet start to give up. But I still can walk; I use a Rollator, you know, the walker with the rolling wheels, the rolling walker. It helps me stay upright when moving and helps me to be mobile.

CK: *When do you use this walker?*

N: When my husband and I take longer walks, I use that because that makes me less tired. This is different than when I tutor; I use a cane at the school. I'm there once a week and always use my cane instead. But at home is different. I can generally get around without using the cane, which sometimes means hanging on to the walls [*laughs*] and I think this is due to the familiarity with my home. I have this same feeling in my son and daughter's houses and have little need for assistance getting around because I am familiar with the homes' environment. When I'm out in public in an unfamiliar place, I have to use at least the cane. I digress a little bit [*laughs*].

CK: *How do you manoeuvre in public spaces?*

N: Well, it's more difficult to be in crowded places because I mean that's more difficult to actually physically kind of get around. And I do rely on my cane, because just to help me walk. It's difficult to kind of just stand and not know there is a wall nearby to hold on to, or railing or something. So, I like having that. And I probably avoid, I mean I used to climb stairs just because I thought that was a good way to get exercise, but now, I don't want to fall down the stairs. So, I avoid stairs. I mean if I have my cane or my husband to hold on to, I can do them but yeah, it's something I want to avoid. Another thing I'm thinking about is my husband was hospitalized last year and walking through the parking lot and all through the hospital was like a long hike for me! I did ask the neurologist if I could have the handicap decal for the car and that really is a blessing. I was joking with my grandson because I would always park far away in the parking lot, and he likes to do that. But now I usually park a little closer, or otherwise at a handicap parking to help me. And if I go to the store, I will usually get a cart from the cart corral in the parking lot and push that in and that helps.

CK: *Do you bring your cane to the stores? What about other travelling methods?*

N: I use the cane to get to the cart then I use the cart. I then put the cane in the cart. Sort of my system. But I think no I probably wouldn't be as comfortable on a train because I haven't been on in some time. I haven't thought about flying; I don't know, like having to manoeuvre to get into the bathroom and I do think about using a handicap stall in the bathroom. And I haven't gotten to the point yet of using my walker when I go to tutor. I haven't because I want to use it less than my cane. I haven't gotten there yet.

CK: *Let's talk about your journey. When were you diagnosed?*

N: Well, I knew I had it long before getting an official diagnosis, but I was officially diagnosed in March 2014. My mother had it, we have a hereditary strain. It has a 50% chance of being passed on to the next generation. My first look at ataxia was through my mother. The whole time as it progressed with my mother, and the last six years of her life she was in a nursing home because she really couldn't take care of herself. Couldn't walk and it became difficult for me to do some of those things with her, or for her, so she and my sister and I put her in a nursing home, but I never worried that am I going to have this ataxia at the time. It wasn't until a few things were off in me that I started to wonder. A few years before getting diagnosed, my family doctor suggested I see a neurologist because when doing my basic physical, he noticed some things that might warrant some further checking by a specialist. So, I went to a neurologist. I tried to get the same neurologist my mother had, but she was unfortunately too busy, so I saw someone else. During this first visit, the neurologist noticed certain basic things, but she didn't give me any sort of diagnosis or anything for that matter. I talked about my family's history and the concerns I had. She suggested that it might be advisable to see a genetic counsellor due to my history.

CK: *Did the genetic counsellor give you a diagnosis?*

N: Eventually, yes. But this was a difficult time for me and a big decision. The benefit is that with a genetic counsellor, you go through the testing and figure out what's wrong with you. But the moment you get that diagnosis, it becomes real. After that diagnosis, I knew that if I fell or had an issue, it would be because I had this ataxia and there was nothing, I could do about it, as there is no cure. So, when the genetic testing was brought up, I didn't do anything about it. By not getting tested right away, it helped to process all of these, all of the changes. As time went on, I seemed to develop more symptoms and then thought maybe I should see the neurologist again to just talk and listen to her advice.

CK: *How did that appointment go?*

N: I talked with her about how I was becoming more aware of some symptoms and again she thought, well, maybe the best thing to do was to see a genetic counsellor. I had processed enough at that time, especially because my mother's type of ataxia is hereditary, not from having a stroke or negative reactions to medications or something like that. Anyway, then after meeting with the neurologist again, my husband and I did go see a genetic counsellor. We talked about my concerns, that I do have this genetic ataxia, and that all I could do was kind of learn to live with it, and that maybe if I did have the genetic test, that would kind of make me almost too, uh, I don't know, too frightened that I did have it and I couldn't change that diagnosis.

CK: *It would become real?*

N: Yes, it became real from that test, even though I already knew I had it. I was still unsure about getting the testing done, so my husband and I decided, OK, we'll just keep at, you know, keep doing things how they currently are. Well, then, I was beginning to see even more symptoms. I became increasingly anxious with the symptoms and eventually caved. I thought, well, maybe it's time. Maybe if I do have it, at least it's confirmed. Then I'll learn to live with it again, but I would at least have that confirmation that it's truly there.

CK: *What steps did you take next?*

N: So, then I went back to meeting with the neurologist. I told her that I was ready to do the genetic test. And kind of wishy washy when I say it out loud like this [*laughs*]. So, then I had the test and it was confirmed and here I am with it today.

CK: *What do you do today for your ataxia?*

N: I see my neurologist every eight to nine months. When I was genetically diagnosed with it, she suggested that I take [medicine] which people with Parkinson's take because it seems to help with balance. So, I do take 100 ml of [medicine] every morning, and she has also recommended some physical therapy. I have gone to physical therapy sessions these past couple of years. The therapists there are familiar with neurological types of conditions and that's been really helpful. They also taught me that ataxia isn't always hereditary, and I guess I wasn't aware that there were people that can develop a nongenetic type of ataxia, and that they have the same struggles. The therapy is mainly to help me just stay active. This is something everyone with ataxia tries to do: stay active. Working on things like balance or flexibility, which is something I think for every age, irrespective of medical condition, is good to do anyway. It's really wonderful [*laughs*]. I'm very impressed. I think I had a six-week session probably about a year ago, and the therapist thought maybe I might be a good candidate for the stack programme, which is a programme that helps people who have gone through therapy to become familiar with some of the equipment at a fitness centre, like some of the weights or maybe how to tell if the treadmill is good or the bikes, or something like that.

CK: *What was your experience working in these programmes?*

N: So, I got to go to the eight-week step programme a couple of years ago, after I finished the therapy. And then last year I actually got to go to two of the step programmes! And that was very good. I have since progressed where some of the equipment are not as good for me. It's better, I think, if I just do some of the slow walking on the treadmill. The treadmill is sometimes a little more difficult to get on and off, which seems silly, but is one of the symptoms of the disease. I noticed the machine is just a short stoop where you need to lift your foot up and get on. But this is very difficult for me to do because I kind of have to retrain my brain, my cerebellum, to lift my foot; and tell myself: 'Nancy, you can get on that.' If it is just even the slightest bit too tall and I don't have anything to hold on to, it just throws me off. But anyway, I was still doing work on exercise equipment for a couple of years. Before that, my husband and I were at the [fitness centre] and would go there, but I'm not as comfortable with that anymore. I still stay active though.

CK: *What is your current activity goal?*

N: Just if I can keep myself just walking, just walking as much as possible. We have since just recently joined the [fitness centre] real close to where we live because we are going, we want to, try the pool that you can just kind of walk into and see if that will help me to do some exercising in the pool. So, we're going to try that [*laughs*].

CK: *Is this something that others can participate in with you?*

N: Yes, and we have an ataxia support group that we have become a part of, and it just started oh, last year, sometime. And one of the ladies that comes was talking about how much comfortable she really is in the pool. As long as you have a pool where you have the stairs and the handle railing that you can hold on to, she can get into the pool comfortably. The [fitness centre] has that and, of course, the [fitness centre] also has the pool you can walk right into. So that inspired me and my husband because he was worried about me to really try the pool like that again. And actually, she also talked about one of those huge adult trikes! My husband and I went to look into one so I'm thinking maybe [*laughs*] all these things I thought 'oh I don't know if I'd ever do that', but no, I'm thinking that if it can keep me mobile, then that might not be bad [*laughs*]. So anyway, those are things that were considered that we're really seriously considering as living with this.

CK: *What about the mobility in your home?*

N: A year ago we moved from our house in [city] that we lived in for forty-three years. We had stairs and a basement that we used regularly in our home, our former house, and I would hold on to the railing whenever I went in the basement. As my symptoms progressed, I would not run up and down the stairs any longer, so I think I was trying to be a little more cautious. Probably not intentional enough. It was interesting, at the same time, I mean, I turned sixty-nine, and so and there's a lot of what's been going on, it is a part of the ageing process also. It's sort of magnified a little bit for me and may be coming sooner than I would like it to.

CK: *Can you talk a little more about balancing those experiences?*

N: I mean there are some balance issues when one gets older and one maybe doesn't walk quite as quickly, or one needs to be careful about falls. People with ataxia have the same concerns everyone will face as they age, it's just that you experience these health and mobility problems just much sooner because of the ataxia. I think we always try to not have a lot of loose rugs around or things in the way that might trip us, but a lot of that wasn't because I was thinking of, you know, of this ataxia. So, we ended up moving to this single story and it's a 55-and-over community, which I have to get used to that. But anyway, the good thing about it is that it is a very open concept and is very low maintenance and the doorways are wide enough so that you could get a wheelchair easily through.

CK: *What was the moving experience like?*

N: So that was, it was very difficult to come to the decision to move, and once we made the decision, it was just great. Actually, it was the neurologist that I was talking with you about regarding my concerns who advised us to move. I asked her what I could do. I wanted to know from her where I could, sort of, have some control over something. One of the ideas she mentioned was to take this decision to move. You know, I kind of thought about it, and our children wanted us to move anyway. They wanted us supported. So anyway, here we are. I don't know if that is more than you wanted [*laughs*].

CK: *So, the move has had a positive impact?*

N: I mean, it's just wonderful what has happened to us this past year or so; the move has been so freeing, because I mean I can really get around our home well. The move has also put us very close to our daughter and her family. And that's been really fun, and well, everything else is well, and everyone else is well, and my husband is supportive, and having the neurologist is helpful, and I have since connected because now I am finding out that there are more studies out there and trials available for me that might help me out.

CK: *What is your experience with doing these trials and studies?*

N: Someone in the previous support group that I had connected with online had talked about a neurologist at the University of Chicago whose speciality and passion is just ataxia. And we also have a friend, a long-time friend, who works there, so I contacted her, and she knew of this doctor. So, then I emailed the doctor and said that because I was in [city], I would be willing to participate in some studies or trials when he had them available. And he responded right away! And he said that sounds wonderful, and he would like to meet me and do an exam first. So, we went to meet with this doctor, and that's been a real positive connection. He wanted to see me again in last November, and at that time he gave me the exam and he's also beginning a study, so I participated in that and I'm going again this May to participate so I know, you know, I asked the neurologist if they are OK with all these involvements, and I probably need to go back to just one doctor [*laughs*]. My neurologist here in Indiana, she is a young lady who I find very supportive. She's again, you know, there isn't a magic pill to give you, or a magic treatment, but her focus on trying to connect me has been really good and trying to remind me, just the way she is, to get focused on what I still am able to do and not focus on what I cannot do, and I just I like that.

CK: *Have you made any other lifestyle changes?*

N: Well I think no, I don't think so, I think my husband has been more concerned that I be careful and do whatever I can to avoid falls. Things like don't carry too much and try to focus on walking and what I'm doing rather than three things at the same time. This was before I knew I had it. I think maybe sometimes I would think, you know, maybe I could have it, but it wasn't something I worried about until when I started to have more symptoms and this was after my mother died and then I thought, maybe now I do need to see a neurologist and again my family doctor thinking it might not hurt to be seen by a neurologist. I started to really deal with it then.

CK: *Sorry to hear about your mom. What was her experience like?*

N: She was diagnosed, around the early 1990s. Maybe, 1991, I can't quite remember. She died in 2008. That's almost seventeen years, and she was eighty-six, so she was, and I may have some of that incorrectly, it might be more mid-1990s for her diagnosis. But she had regularly seen an eye doctor and on the one visit with an eye doctor, the eye doctor thought that she needed to see an eye specialist; there was something that he noticed that needed some further examining. She also was having some difficulty. My mother had earlier on, an issue with the part of the eardrum that needed to be removed and that was replaced with an artificial thing. There were some balance issues and also, gosh long time ago. I think I was in junior high school; she broke her neck, in a fall. So, some of her coordination and balance issues related to this fall, and some issues with, you know, her inner ear. But then she went to the eye specialist, and they thought it was more neurological, and the eye specialist recommended the neurologist. Anyway, the neurologist that she saw then, diagnosed her with this ataxia. When my mother was diagnosed there was so little known about it, ataxia, that now, gosh, we're finding out that there are so many different kinds that they're both genetic and related to, you know, having a stroke or perhaps some medication treatment issues, like that. Every once in a while, when my sister and I would both take my mother to the neurologist appointment, the neurologist would do a very brief exam. The exam that he does for neurological testing and then says oh you don't have it, or he would say to my mother, 'now don't worry because when your daughters are older, they will have a cure', so you know. That was kind of the only conversation that we had with this whole genetic line so to speak [*laughs*].

CK: *When she was diagnosed, was there any source of information to learn more about ataxia?*

N: No, no, there were just some very basic research when my mother was diagnosed, and, I mean, it was very limited. So that it never really led to much more. The ataxia that I have SCA 3, is also known as Machado-Joseph disease.

CK: *How did you find out this other name for it?*

N: I can remember when one of the psychology classes I took in college there was this very brief mention of this disease and I don't know how it was, I don't remember how it was mentioned other than as a rare genetic neurological disease. And since this ataxia was very rare, there was no cure; there wasn't much really to find out. And it was really later on that we did more research and discovered that Machado-Joseph disease can be traced to Portugal and that there was a higher incident there, so there didn't seem to be a whole lot of information. Though I think deep down, I just didn't want to sulk about being consumed by this because I thought if I am consumed by it, that's going to make my whole identity just ataxia, and there so much more else to life. Yet now I'm finding not that it's consuming but maybe it's more real and I'm living with it in mind, and not going to deny it, and live with it, and just be my own person. So, I don't know if that answered you question but [*laughs*].

CK: *What was your experience sharing this diagnosis with your family?*

N: My husband was with me in the neurology appointment, so that was something that we just talked about all along, and to our children, yes, our daughter and then to our son that yes, I have it, and I'm just going to learn to live with it and then to my sister. I told them that with this ataxia, there is a 50% chance that we'll get it if a parent has it. If I were not, if I had not gotten it, then our children are off the hook, you know, that's OK, they won't get it. But now there's a 50% chance that either one of them, I guess both of them, could get it.

CK: *What about for your mental health? What was that experience like?*

N: So, it's never really, I mean nothing was hidden, and it's just kind of, I have it and I'm hoping to learn to live with it. I'm hoping to remain positive about life because there are just so many other good things to be thankful for and grateful for. That worked until near the end of 2015. I found that I was starting to get depressed. It's that I think it was because I was going through the grief process of receiving not a terminal illness, but receiving something that I didn't want to receive, and that there wasn't anything I could do about it. Because there isn't a cure, there isn't a magic pill that will make it go away.

CK: *What happened during that period of time?*

N: So, then I did, it became a really stressful time for my family because my, prior to that, my mother-in-law's husband passed and she was going through, um, that. Well, uh, some uh, physical illness and probably started having depression with that, and it was a really difficult time. My husband, he wanted to, and I wanted him to help her with her affairs. She was just not able to do anything. And then she was living in northern Indiana and she couldn't decide whether to live closer to us here. At that time, my husband's sister also lived here, so there were a lot of challenges for him. Anyway, that was a difficult time.

CK: *How did you take care of yourself?*

N: Without digressing into all of that, when I saw my neurologist, I did share with her that it seems as if I was depressed and she suggested an antidepressant which she told me, you know, to try it and I said I would. I gave it a week and I just didn't like it; I felt like I was not at all a part of me. I went to see a counsellor and that was very helpful.

CK: *What was your experience with the counsellor like?*

N: I didn't see this counsellor very long, but I found it was very helpful and it seemed to help me get back on track and I think that acknowledging that it was grieving process that I was experiencing helped a lot. Because I thought of it as grief for me because it was the losing of what I loved to do. Because I love to walk and not like a power walker, but I love to walk. Like my husband and I got to a point where we retired and if we have a chance, if we are driving somewhere, we just stop and walk for a bit. It was nice. But walking had just become cumbersome. So now I just think going through all of that, that sadness, then being able to get the help to come to grips with it was hard. I realized that it was not nearly the end of life and that there are lots of other people that have to go through a lot of more horrible things and focusing on what I can be grateful for rather than what I can't do or just pity myself for helped considerably.

CK: *That's really inspiring to hear you pushed through.*

N: Well, thank you, it's not always that way. There are sometimes I do get discouraged. But there are just, it was very helpful to see the counsellor to help me get back on track.

CK: What advice would you give to other individuals who are beginning their journey with ataxia?

N: That's a good question [*laughs*]. I think to be connected to a neurologist that wants to help or be connected with some support groups. I think these are very helpful and I'm finding that a support group is helpful so that it doesn't seem like you're the only one who has this thing that very few people have heard of. It can be lonely to have a disease that only a few neurologists know about. But I think I'm at a point in my life that is so different because when I think back to my mother, people just, you know, didn't know about ataxia and I think it's probably only neurologists, and probably, maybe, those that are really teaching their research to get the word out there. If not, I think it's just, you know, it would be really isolating to not have that support and so, for my mother, she connected with a neurologist just because she found that the neurologist answered very kindly and there was just really a bond. And that connected for me. I feel like I have that but now there is more publicity about it. The fact that I'm talking to you, you know, is a good thing. There's a lot of hope.

After finishing the interview questions, Nancy and I talked a little more about my connection to the ataxia community as well as her future goals for the Indiana groups. As I could feel the conversation ending, I was struck with a sudden sense of sadness. After hearing her struggles and triumphs, I knew there was so much more for her to tell.

Before I could send a follow-up message, I was surprised to see that Nancy had already messaged me. This simple note thanked me for talking with her and included additional information about the support group and the activities they do. Because of this, I talked with her about staying in contact and I have been welcomed into the support group.

Nancy's ataxia journey is unique and yet shares commonalities with many individuals who have ataxia in Indiana. Many of these individuals face the same milestones she has and have a fire of hope in their hearts. Through awareness, education, and research, we will be one step closer to a cure.

Lisa's Story

Background

The sun shyly peered through the window, highlighting the interview question sheet in front of me. I read through the questions for the hundredth time in the sunlight, ensuring I was prepared for the upcoming interview. The familiar excitement gripped my being as I silenced my 9 AM alarm reminder. Today I would be talking with Lisa, a very passionate member of the ataxia community. My hurriedly scribbled notes reminded me that she was in her fifties and over a decade into her ataxia journey. With the support of her family, she had been able to overcome many milestones related to her physical and mental health and wellbeing. She is the mother of three children, all adults who had left home by the time of the interview. Lisa values the importance of visibility for Ataxia and is a vocal member of the ataxia community whose aim is to educate others (the general public).

As my final alarm went off, I dialled her number and heard the first ring. Before the second ring could finish, a voice called out from the line. It was Lisa's husband, who is also her primary caregiver. We had a brief conversation and I learned that Lisa was working on organizing a new fundraiser. Lisa eventually popped on the line, and so the interview began.

Cassie Kresnye: What started you on your ataxia journey?

Lisa: Before I knew, I blamed everything on my knee. You see, I had ACL [anterior cruciate ligament] surgery, a reconstruction. I was horseback riding, and I was thrown into a jump, and that hurt my ACL in 1997. At the time, I didn't get it fixed. About five years later, I was with my daughter delivering Girl Scout cookies and we dropped something off across the street. There were brand new neighbours that just moved in and my daughter automatically put her arm out to give me some balance going down their front stairs because there was no handrail. Out of habit, I blamed my lack of coordination on my knee as I didn't know another reason why. But I knew something was not right.

CK: *What did you do?*

L: I became more aware of the changes. I noticed several things, especially how my family interacted with me. It almost became a norm it seemed, where they would automatically aid when I moved around. For example, I took my son to the zoo as a chaperone with his class and they had multiple levels throughout the area. Every time there was a step down it was just natural for him to come over and give me his arm, I never asked for it once.

CK: *So, the family began to support you more?*

L: Correct, it was just something that the family always did. Absolutely. This tipped me off that I needed to get the red herring knee fixed. I started the process of getting surgery done in 2003. It was a long process, and hard on the family as the kids were still in the house and I wasn't allowed to drive. So, a lot fell on my husband then, and I'm very grateful for what he did. Even then he was a great caregiver. He even put up with my parent's giving me a bell to ring when I needed him [*laughs*]. I still have the bell too!

CK: *Did your recovery go smoothly?*

L: With my husband, absolutely. With his help and my determination, I was up and walking around before I knew it. Unfortunately, we noticed soon that even with the fixed ACL something was still not right. I know now that my ataxia symptoms really ramped up then. So, the first thing that I did was to call an orthopaedic surgeon. His office said before I could speak with him, I needed to have a gait study done. Just to see why, or to decide as to why I walked the way I did, especially given the recent surgery.

CK: *What was that study like?*

L: It was probably about half an hour, and in front of an orthopaedic surgeon. He asked me to walk normally around the room as well as do different movements such as crouching down into a squat and standing back up. Those crouching activities were difficult, as you need good balance for them. I tried my best to do them, but I ran into the wall over and over. To my surprise, the orthopaedic surgeon said my knees were structurally sound and that my difficulty is most likely neurological. I was shocked.

CK: *What did you do after that?*

L: I went home. I had no idea what to do, as our family had no history of neurological disorders. I started to think more about my younger days, to see if there were any clues then that I missed.

CK: *What did you think about?*

L: I was busy, I was very active when I was younger. I never ever thought that anything was wrong because I was so active. When I was doing things, I didn't know anything different, it was just one of those things that happened to me. I never once wondered why things where so difficult for me because they seemed so easy for everyone else. For example, in horseback riding, you use a lot of leg muscles. I specifically had to think of that exact muscle, and I had to almost physically concentrate on that particular thing. Multitasking it not something I am good at; I've never been good at it. I also never had good balance.

CK: *Did your parents ever notice any differences?*

L: My parents believed that I was just a natural klutz, a childhood quirk. No one had ever heard of ataxia and my quirk seemed to simply be a coordination issue I would grow out of. It was just understood by pretty much everyone around me that I didn't have any balance. I'm not certain if they thought more of it. I mean if they were concerned, if it were completely out of the ordinary, I would have been checked out. But it really wasn't, ataxia can be tricky like that when you're younger. I also think that the difficulties I was having were what was normal, so they didn't have anything to worry about. It was just the way it was. There wasn't a question or anything.

CK: *How about your teenage years? Any clues then?*

L: I have memories back to when I was a teenager to when I believe I was fifteen years old. I wasn't old enough to be working, however, I put a lot of effort into making pizza dough at a master pizza shop. Because this job was very busy on a particular day, I was asked to take a tray of six water tumblers. It was about 20 feet over to the table. Seems like it was not that difficult; however, I took one step and the water sloshed everywhere. Looking back now, I'm surprised they even let me try to get the water to the table.

CK: *Did your primary doctor ever mention anything to you?*

L: I mean I never knew there was an issue, even when I went to a check-up each year. I actually had a horrible migraine a few days after the gait study and tried to get an appointment with my primary doctor. These migraines were something I've always gotten since I was young. After calling, I was told that at that point in time unless I am symptomatic, I cannot go see her, I have to make an appointment with a different doctor. That kind of irritated me, at least the way I was feeling with my emotions everywhere. At the time, I didn't believe it would be safe for me to get behind the wheel of the car, which should have been enough of a symptom. But anyway, I said 'no' to an appointment with a random doctor and called up another doctor I knew; she was an osteopathic doctor.

CK: *Did you get an appointment with her?*

L: She got me in that day. She read through my file, read through everything, and one of the items in my file was the gait study I did a few days before. She saw the doctor said my knees were completely fine. That's when she asked me to just walk for a little distance in the examination room and then she immediately recommended a brain MRI. And that is where everything began because my results in the MRI were very different than what anyone would normally think. She also recommended to make an appointment with a neurological doctor. I was referred to a doctor that was within the same clinic, and when I went there, the neurological doctor gave me a simple hand eye coordination test. She said: 'I'm going to move my finger from left to right and I want you to follow my finger with your eyes, don't move your head or anything else.' After I did that one exercise, that's when the doctor said "Have you never seen a doctor?" and of course I asked why, and she said from what she did, one exercise, she could tell I did not have full control of my eyes.

CK: *She knew from one activity?*

L: She said, 'eyes don't lie' and I did not have full power to use them. My eyes do things that they want, and the doctor said that its part of a syndrome. She told me that when my eyes shaking back and forth, it is a condition called nystagmus, and it is definitely a calling card for something else.

CK: *Did she check any other symptoms?*

L: I was sitting on the bench, and she pushed my arm a little bit. Instead of moving away from her, my reaction was to move into her. Which is another symptom of the same syndrome that people suffering from nystagmus have. After this appointment, it took a couple more before I learned about my exact diagnosis. You see, that's the hard thing about ataxia, a doctor can't diagnose you with one symptom as it is several put together and that takes time. It's only when you confirm the set that you know what you have. In this particular appointment, I was told that I had ataxia due to cerebellum atrophy. My first question I had was 'what is that?' Now most people, including myself and my husband, had never heard of ataxia before. Ataxia was so rare that the doctor didn't even know what to do with me. I do appreciate that she was honest, saying she had only read about it in medical school. I suppose I was a textbook case, literally [*laughs*]. My husband and I went home, and those days were hard.

CK: *What did you do once you were home?*

L: Well, it didn't feel real at first, but I had to know more. I learned why it is so hard to diagnose it, as it's not even a disease at all, it's a set of symptoms. It's Greek that translates to 'lack of coordination'. I learned that I probably had the genetic version. After searching and searching, I came upon a terrible conclusion. Ataxia has no cure, not even an effective treatment. And it's so rare that it can be difficult to study. But it really isn't that rare, just misdiagnosed. Its symptoms are so similar to Parkinson's, MS and ALS [multiple sclerosis and a torn anterior cruciate ligament], those are all very close cousins of ataxia and those are more mainstream than ataxia would be. However, it is estimated that 1 in 100,000 people have ataxia. That might sound small, but in terms of billions of people that's huge. So, it's grossly underdiagnosed. The worst realization was that after all this time of figuring out what's wrong, I finally learned a name but could do nothing about it. I saw countless physical therapy videos of 'normal' people standing with their feet together, at that point in time I could not do that, my feet where at least 10 inches apart. I spiralled down a rabbit whole of worst-case scenario research on Google and became physically ill from what I was reading. Because of this, my husband and I decided that I will not Google the disorder for a while until we have a better understanding from the doctor.

CK: *Did you ever hear from the doctor again?*

L: Three days later, the doctor's office called with the next steps and asked me if I could go to the lab at my earliest convenience because I needed to have blood tests done. And that's when everything started to roll along; when my battle with whatever was wrong with me began. It really did start making sense the more I dug into it. Indeed, I was stunned nothing was noticed before. Anyway, the doctor sent me to the lab for blood tests and for genetic testing because she wanted to know what kind of ataxia that she was dealing with. I won't sugar-coat it, the genetic testing is expensive, especially back then. It's dropped a little now, but it's a major decision to have it done.

CK: Was the blood test the confirmation?

L: Obviously in my blood she found that there was a genetic base to my ataxia. She came back and told me it was hereditary and what I need to do. Turned out I needed to see an even more specialized neurologist doctor. I needed to go to a specific ataxia doctor. Those are very hard to find; I could probably count, off my fingers, the number of specialists in the United States.

CK: *How did you handle having an official diagnosis?*

L: In my family, I shared. I asked my sister-in-law; she is a medical assistant that works in a doctor's office. I called her and I asked her what the doctors there recommended for me. She got back to me very quickly because when she said ataxia, the doctors in her office listened. They didn't tell her they needed to hang on and they would get back to her after they did research. No, when she said my sister-in-law was just diagnosed with ataxia, they instantly said that what I needed to do was to go to a hospital where they had a specific ataxia unit, or to a hospital where they had an ataxia wing. They instantly said that I needed a specialist of specialists because there are not many people or doctors who knew what ataxia was or what the symptoms of it were, because the symptoms mimicked other disorders like I said before.

CK: *Did you find an ataxia doctor?*

L: Yes, they recommended [doctor]. He has an entire ataxia unit. Now that was a challenge in of itself, as the doctor did not just take on new patients. I called his office and I was told that I was to send a copy of my brain MRI as well as my records pertaining to this syndrome and he would take a look at it. Then he would then let me know if he wanted to see me or if he thought seeing someone else would benefit me more. Now that was in February 2011. He eventually did see me and continues to see me.

CK: *What was it like to finally see the specialist?*

L: It was a step. Because I have a genetic strand, he said I had had it my whole life. He told me he had similar patients who blamed other injuries, like I did with my knee. It's typical of an ataxic, he said. What I loved most is that he really listened to me, not just told me what's wrong with me. He answered any concerns I had and was honest about the current limitations of research.

CK: *Now that you found your new doctor, what were your next steps?*

L: So, the diagnosis and new doctor did change my family life a bit. Now that we had a name, I was pretty much under a microscope around my family for any symptoms. If they saw something about me, I needed to write it down, so I could ask the doctor and see if perhaps that was part of the syndrome that I had. Again, the doctor is one of the only doctors that I had seen for ataxia who was really more interested in speaking with me. Other doctors tended to be harder to talk about my symptoms, especially the more specialized they were, with only one of them ever admitting they didn't know what it was.

CK: *Where did you look to for support now you had an official diagnosis?*

L: Well, first no one. Ataxia is a very solitary disorder, as it's hard to find others with it for support. I had my family, but it took years and years to finally accept the fact that I had this disorder. Because of this, I was in no place to talk to strangers about it. I did slowly grow more comfortable with the idea, but definitely relied on the bad knee excuse a little too often. I did eventually start telling friends, but not without issues. The first issue to come up was what I call 'the look' when you tell someone you have an incurable condition. Why do people instantly feel sorry for me? I am still the exact same person, I'm still here inside. Just because I have a disorder that does not mean that I have diminished as a person at all. The day I was diagnosed, and even 10 minutes after that, I was not any different than before I was diagnosed. Sure, they put a name on me; they labelled a syndrome on me, but they didn't change me as a person. The other issue was that they didn't really understand me. I like to think ataxia is like a broken arm.

CK: *How so?*

L: If you have a broken arm, people see your cast and give you empathy. But unless they have had a broken arm as well, they really don't know what you're going through. I'm lucky enough to not need a physical apparatus, but many people with ataxia need them and just like a cast can't really hide it. So, they have to deal with the pity looks. Tired of 'the look', I did eventually find a support group. My physical therapist found a group, the National Ataxia Foundation, but they go by NAF. It has been around for a while, and it has both researchers looking into the disorder as well as patients and their families attending their meetings. I thought this was amazing, that the NAF meeting gave patients an opportunity to talk about their questions and concerns. I found a lot of information on their website, including local support groups.

CK: *Did you end up going to a support group meeting?*

L: Yes! In my group there was one lady who believed that she was the only person who had ataxia because she never heard of it, neither did anyone around her. She talked about how lonely she felt, and I immediately connected with her. I knew that feeling, because while my family tried, they didn't have the disorder, they didn't know what it was really like. She helped me a lot, especially with places to look for information that wasn't worst case scenario. That's how I started doing exercises to maintain what little coordination I had [*laughs*].

CK: So, the group had a positive effect on your journey?

L: Oh yes absolutely. I did eventually start attending the annual meeting of NAF too, and those are special. The meetings are made of people who have ataxia and researchers who understand every single aspect of it, and they can point you in the right direction. There really is nothing like having someone that completely understands what you are going through today, not to mention those that can advise your tomorrow too. And I think that the most important thing is to have someone that understands what is happening to you or what could possibly happen to you in the future.

CK: What is it like being at the annual meeting?

L: The best way I can put it is a wonderful escape. It is a wonderful escape being in a room with people that completely understand what is going on with you. It is a wonderful feeling of walking across a room and not being judged. I already know that I may not walk completely normal; however, if I stumble, I do not have the entire room stop and stare at me because these people understand. It is understood that if you need help, ask for it, it's right there, it is all around you.

CK: What made this help different?

L: When you are in that room with a bunch of people who share the disorder, they understand the point where someone needs help. We are not afraid to say it, sometimes when people want to help you, people specifically without understanding ataxia, they are going overboard to try and help you, and this is not something that is comforting because that gesture of wanting to help draws attention and that is something that most people with ataxia are afraid of. But not in this room, they know how to help each other in a way that does not draw attention. And even if attention is drawn, you don't feel embarrassed, as they all understand, you don't have to explain yourself.

CK: What is your favourite part of the meeting?

L: Without a doubt, the dancing party. Sounds crazy right? A bunch of people who don't have great motion dancing, huh. But it's the most freeing part of the meeting. I used to dance with my husband, just some ballroom classes we took, but stopped once my condition progressed. I became shy almost, afraid of the lack of control I had. But this dancing is different. There is no judgement here, this dancing is for people with ataxia.

CK: That's wonderful to hear.

L: I always see smiles on everyone's faces as they dance freely, not worrying about how they look. It's the happiest moment of their year, you know. For a couple hours they don't have to worry about ataxia, they can just be themselves and have a good time. It's really magical.

CK: *Where is the meeting held?*

L: Oh, it changes each year. Different places each time. But it does have an issue, the hotel. NAF encourages people who have ataxia specifically to go there. Well, hotels are nice, but only have a few rooms that are handicap accessible. So that means a lot of the handicapped people that are attending the same conference need to stay in other places because their needs cannot be accommodated, or they have to deal with the nonhandicap rooms. It can be hard on them.

CK: *What other issues do you face in public areas?*

L: One of my worst fears is going down steps. A large part of this syndrome is a balance issue. The biggest fear I have is going downstairs simply because it requires coordination of several muscles. For a 'normal' person most people will just go down steps and not even think about it. But me? I have to think 'OK, I need to lean back because my centre of gravity needs to be over my feet. OK, I need to bend one knee while I am lowering my body from the step above; I need to make sure my foot is straight on the step, because if it is skewed, my balance will be going in that direction'. I need to visualize, and I need to specifically think about what I need to do in order to get down the stairs. Now there are several houses and mine is included that are not accessible without going down steps or up steps. And that is a huge issue in a lot of places. But I think it's important to face what you are afraid of and find a way to do things. My perspective is the fact that I do not have a disability, I simply have a different ability. I may not do things as in going up and down steps the same way a 'normal' person does, but I do go up and down steps. However, if there is an alternative ramp available, my husband or family will ask if I want help going down the step or if I want to go to a ramp.

CK: *Are you comfortable using escalators?*

L: In places like airports, they have elevators, but they also have escalators and that means I simply need to get my foot on to one step and then it will take me down the stairs. That's typically a very good choice for me. If I'm carrying a bag or anything, an elevator is better since it's easier to lose my balance when holding stuff. Not to say I haven't fallen trying, however. I have fallen pretty much on any surface known to man. The difference between myself and somebody else is the fact that I know how to fall. I've fallen so much so I know how not to get hurt. That's not necessarily a good thing; however, it is truth that I work with.

CK: *Are there any other issues?*

L: The last one I can think of is the fact it's a solitary disorder, and I have issues speaking to large groups. For example, when I was in [city] I needed to address a large group involving ataxia awareness. Being that I have ataxia, I believe very strongly in increasing awareness to help people diagnose it early and inform those that have it of their resources. But because of the years of being concerned about how odd I looked when I move, I was terrified of having hundreds of eyes on me. That's a thing about having ataxia, you just want to fade into the background sometimes as the constant worrying about what others think is draining.

CK: *What do you do when these issues pop up together?*

L: It depends. For example, at the zoo when you go to certain exhibits, if it involves a step, as well as larger groups of people, I shied away from that. Because we are gradually finding out more and more that there is an emotional aspect to this disorder and no one wants to be labelled as having something wrong with them, it is much easier to simply avoid being noticed, and not fall in front of them. But I'm lucky that I can choose to disappear, as I do not have a physical apparatus as many people with ataxia have. However, sometimes I can't disappear. When I'm in a public place, if I see steps as well as a group of people, then I need to come up with some plan. I have to prioritize what my fears or disabilities are. So, which is more important, my fear of going down steps or my fear of crowded places? That's personally exactly what I have to do because I know both things are there, and I know that I need to get through these things. So that's when I needed to start thinking about how I am going to do just that. You can throw a third issue in and that is the issue if someone bumps into me. Like I said before with my doctor, instead of moving away from them I go back to them. So how do I get from point A to point B while going down steps into a crowd of people as well as having these people bump into me? This can be overwhelming. When this happens, I all of the sudden completely freeze up, because when I'm thinking 'oh my gosh oh jeez, I have to go on steps', I'll work myself up into a frenzy. It's something that you either go through or go around.

CK: *What do you do when this happens?*

L: Well, I don't always go straight through and run into or go against my fears. No, it's usually the path of least resistance. What I personally do is to say something like 'I'm out in public; there are people there; OK', there are times when I am so afraid that I really do not want to put myself in the middle of a more fearful situation. So even though it takes me twice as long, I'm going to go around it and I'm going to avoid it in any way possible. That again is a choice that I make because there are days that the fight is in me, but there are other days where I am sick and tired of being afraid, and those are the days when I do not want to deal with anything or anyone. But that doesn't mean always avoiding the fear or fight. When I have the strength, I will face it head on even though it can be really scary.

Conclusion

Once I ended the recording, Lisa and I talked for a couple of minutes before she had to get back to her day job. However, her real job was actively working towards spreading awareness. Through social media, legislation and organizing fundraisers, she works constantly to inform others and support them in their journeys. Inspired by our conversations, I was able to attend the conference she discussed, particularly the dance party, and was able to experience the few hours of pure judgement-free bliss Lisa talked about. It was truly magical to see hundreds of faces light up as everyone came together to focus on a shared physical activity without fear of being judged. The room was filled with laughter and squeals and continues to be a highly anticipated event for conference attendees.

Lisa's ataxia journey is one that is constantly changing, bending around curves and persevering through mountains of difficulties. This journey is shared by many individuals with ataxia and, in Lisa's experience, is made stronger through the sense of community these individuals share. The world has much to learn about this disorder, and researchers are working towards finding the elusive cure. What has been missing thus far has been ears willing and ready to listen to the unique stories of the lived experiences of this unique population. There is no doubt that if society does not pay attention to these stories, it cannot understand the population's special needs. Lack of understanding of their needs consequently makes it impossible to assist them in a manner that is both relevant and adequate. There is no doubt that each day members of the ataxia community, thousands strong, bravely marches on. They face each morning with a fire in their hearts, charging towards the future with unstoppable courage.

Cassie Kresnye is completing a doctorate at Indiana University-Bloomington. Her research interests are in personal informatics with a focus on lifestyle data sources and data mining. As a programmer, she enjoys being an Arduino hobbyist and continues to make interactive toys for companion animals.

Chapter 3

DISCOVERING UNSPOKEN COMMUNICATION
Lived Experiences of a Deaf Person and His Doctor

Mackenzie Jones

Speak your truth clearly; and listen to others; they too have their story.
—Max Ehrmann, 1952

This chapter deals with two narratives: that of a physician who has experience providing care to patients who are deaf/hard of hearing (d/hh) and the lived experiences of a Deaf individual. In the first narrative, Trip, a physician, narrates his experiences in caring for a patient who is Deaf. Trip talks about his background of having a physician father and hence growing up in a home that obviously drew him into medicine. He also talks about his choice of residency and fellowship in medical school. He also mentions about his vague familiarity with American Sign Language (ASL) and how it comes in handy when assisting patients who are Deaf. He details his experiences with patients who are d/hh and how his use of approaches like raising one's voice, sitting in front of a patient to assist in lip reading, and using ASL enables him to communicate and hence care for his patients. In addition, he talks about how the use of a Video Relay System (VRS)[1] and computer monitors on rolling tables has helped with providing appropriate and quality care at the hospital.

The second narrative is that of Adam, a professor of ASL who is Deaf. Adam uses cordial interlocution with his students for his class each morning. His story provides instances of positive and negative interactions with healthcare providers and postulates ideas for providing and ensuring a more equitable healthcare system. His narrative touches on childhood issues, college, and life, as well as the difficulties he had with healthcare affordability and with getting an appropriate job because of employment discrimination against people who are d/hh. He also talks about support he received from home, his family and his colleagues that made managing his hearing loss less stressful.

Caring for the Deaf: A Physician's Experience

Introduction

Trip (TT) is a smaller gentleman who is physically fit, but with an air of shy empathy. He carries himself well and confidently. He did not appear egoistic; I had met him a few times before. He was, in fact, my own doctor and that is why I knew of his experience working with a Deaf patient. As I introduced myself for the first time regarding this project, he inquired about what I was doing in Indiana. My immediate response was 'school, grad school', to be exact. But he didn't stop there; he actually cared and encouraged me to share my interests and my goals for changing the world. I explained my focus on public health and, with it, my desire to improve quality of care for those with disabilities, specifically those with communication disorders such as d/hh populations. It was after hearing the focus of my research that he perked up and expressed his experience with d/hh patients.

Trip was excited to share for a brief moment, and I knew I wanted to hear more of that story, so when I decided to professionally explore narratives and the experience of marginalized populations, a professional space and time had been 'established'. This gave me an unparalleled opportunity to ask him for details regarding his lived experience as a physician serving his fellow humans. For Trip, it meant, among other things, fingerspelling his name despite learning the ASL alphabet about thirty years ago.

On the day of the interview, Trip walked forward to greet me in the lobby as we had set the meeting in a place that was convenient for him. He said 'the hospital' and I responded 'I'll be there', even though I was not entirely sure if our conversation would end up taking place in the operation room. Although not exactly next to the scalpel – or in his case the endoscopy probe – we made ourselves comfortable in the observation room off to the side. He was wearing a T-shirt and scrub trousers. In my time shadowing doctors, thinking I'd be one myself, I learned that this is typical attire for a half-office-half-procedure speciality. Trip is a gastroenterologist, or a digestive tract doctor, and he spends about 70% of his time doing procedures and 30% meeting patients for office appointments. Otolaryngology – ear, nose and throat doctor – is another facet of his 'hybrid' schedule.

Now for this interview, one might have thought I would have wanted an ear, nose and throat doctor, as that would align more with patients who are d/hh. However, I wanted to have the perspective of a general practitioner (i.e. family or internal medicine); one who doesn't have a reputation of working with those who may be d/hh. Thus, the goal of my interview was to understand the communication strategies actually used in a hospital or a doctor's office when a patient is Deaf and to explore the experience of a physician who may not be used to working with Deaf people on a regular basis.

The Americans with Disabilities Act (ADA) has provided guidelines for nondiscriminatory care for those with communication disorders. Title II requires government-run organizations to consider the preferences for communication aids and Title III encourages nonprofit and other businesses to consider their 'preferences'. This means that state and local health clinics must ask their patients who are d/hh what type of aid they believe would provide appropriate and effective communication when seeking healthcare. Where a healthcare facility is private, voluntary or not-for-profit, it must provide some type of aid and not necessarily what is 'preferred' (US Department of Justice: Civil Rights Division 2014). However, the ADA sets expectations for hospitals and smaller health entities to foster effective communication for their patients in order to ensure the highest quality of care in order to provide equal care to them as it does for those without a communication barrier.

I have intentionally emphasized the 'rules' and expectations of the ADA because communication is the most important theme throughout this interview. Trip discusses his personal experiences, but also brings in facts and procedures that are related to the hospital where he works. Although the services may not always be 'the best', it is clear that there is an effort to make things work; facilities had been put in place to foster communication between physicians and their patients, something that did not exist in the past.

In sharing my conversation with Trip, I first and foremost call on the reader to determine the significance of the stories shared. Specifically, by reading both Trip's and Adam's experiences, I urge you (the reader) to discover moments of parallelism (similarity and identicality), overlap and disconnect. I also implore you to consider (or even come up with) solutions to initiate and improve physician–client interaction to ensure effective communication within the overall healthcare setting. This, I believe, will act as a pathfinder for public health professionals, social services providers and other stakeholders to better support physicians in providing much-needed healthcare services to one and all.

Up until now, I have used 'Deaf', 'deaf' and 'hard of hearing' interchangeably and one may be wondering: *are these the same? If they are different, then what is the difference?* The last two – 'deaf' and 'hard of hearing' – refer to the medical condition of having hearing loss as well as to the significance of that loss. When someone is deaf, they typically have severe to profound hearing loss. For someone who is hard of hearing, they tend to have mild to moderate hearing loss. However, both terms are also sometimes used identically, given the fact that the edges of the medical diagnosis may be blurry.

On the other hand, Deaf with a capital 'D' refers to the culture of the Deaf world. One does not have to be deaf to be a part of Deaf culture, as children of deaf adults (CODAs) and interpreters are often included. However, with Deaf, a deep understanding of ritual, traditions and values along with the fluency of ASL is necessary. It is important to note that for linguists, speech pathologists and audiologists, ASL is a distinct language, not a string of signs that symbolize and follow English words and grammar. ASL has its own grammar and much of it is expressed through facial expression (gaze) and gesture (body language). Given my curiosity in the language barrier that exists for those whose primary language is ASL, I have emphasized this individual's experience in the interview. However, Trip does discuss his strategies for communicating with those who are d/hh as well.

As this was my first attempt at a semi-structured interview, I was unsure of what to focus on: among other things, the questions, Trip's face and facial expressions, paper and pencil, my report and/or account of our discourse or his exact words. About 5 minutes into the interview, I realized that paper and pen/pencil were going to be necessary only if I needed to hold on to a thought for follow-up questions. An observation of Trip's face pointed to moments when his eyes 'looked' uncomfortable, despite his tongue and mouth continuing to tell his story. This occurred even more so at a point when I asked about the possibility of his hospital not following the best practices regarding patient communication. But this is not one doctor's problem; it is a health system flaw and acknowledging these incidences is important in reducing the chance of reoccurrence. Trip's story shows honest regret for the times he was not able to support his patients. However, his enthusiasm for the current hospital set-up with computer-based interpreting and his openness to make Deaf patients feel comfortable showed promise for a more culturally competent and caring generation of health providers.

The Story

Trip began by saying that one of the things he tried to do in particular if someone was Deaf (and this went back to his first babysitter who taught him sign language) was to shake hands with them. He noted:

TRIP: I don't remember much about that. I was four years old, but I still know it. What I do when I meet them is, I'll shake their hand and I'll say my name is TS and I will sign my name, so they know. In this last patient experience, he called me out that it was one T, asking me if my name was really one T and if I was missing a T, it's typically two Ts (TT), but I caught what he was saying and I told him it was one T. That's the way I kind of break the ice so to speak for people who have hearing impairments.

The rest of the interaction is given below:

MACKENZIE JONES: *How do you typically feel that comes across?*

T: Oh, I feel it is good. I mean it's nice trying to get on a more even playing field and showing them, you know, I can understand some of what they say – certainly not all of what they are signing. And again, they have a translator; not a translator, but someone to assist, someone who knows sign language...

MJ: *An interpreter?*

T: An interpreter, yeah, that's a good thing. It's about making eye contact with the patient and not making eye contact with the interpreter. That's what you do with the people who have language barriers. You talk to them and the interpreter will communicate if you are making the eye contact. That's what we have been trained to do, is talk to the patient and not the interpreter

MJ: *Can you tell me about the training where you learned that information?*

T: Sure. We have classes on working with patients with disabilities, whether it is, you know, language barriers or in this instance hearing impairments. These are generic classes that encompass multiple things and maybe one or two days are focused on that. And so I wouldn't say it was a whole class, I'd say maybe three hours that was dedicated to it.

MJ: *And are these classes in medical school or through continuing education?*

T: Medical school. I haven't had any new education since medical school, I just learn as I interact with people in the community.

MJ: *Do you remember any hands-on experience with disabilities throughout your training?*

T: You mean an actual patient?

MJ: *Yes, patients.*

T: No, it was more education on how to work with patients, I don't think they brought [people in], I mean they did for some classes. It would be like a physical exam where you come in and see someone that had advanced liver disease and you'd see what their presentation is like, but we didn't have anything like that or any [simulated patients] with any kind of impairments.

MJ: How would you go about approaching a situation with someone who was deaf or hard of hearing and didn't use an interpreter?

T: It usually comes down to raising your voice. Then again sitting in front of them because they have learned to lip read. There's a lot of similarities between hearing impaired and completely deaf and how I approached it. I don't get to do the sign language thing very often with them. But it's just really raising your voice, sometimes tone of voice – women, nurses tend to have a tougher time with hearing impaired as opposed to male voices. I don't know, [I think] it's the tone.

MJ: Have you found that out through experience?

T: Yeah, no education just experience.

MJ: Have you ever talked with other professionals about the experience with deaf or hard of hearing individuals?

T: It's not typical conversation that you would bring up, you typically bring up something that challenges you or that you have questions about. This situation doesn't really present a lot of challenges unless there's nobody to help you to interpret.

MJ: When you go to conferences or you have continuing education, is there any training at all related to either deaf or hard of hearing or disability?

T: No, there is there is . . . no. . .

MJ: No.

T: I wouldn't know if there was anything new unless it was in a visit. It might happen that I didn't know that something existed, and I showed up one day and the hospital was using it. That's how I would find out. There is no continuing education of these new advances in certain areas of communication.

MJ: Do you know if your medical school was ahead of its time in having those cultural classes around disability or is that kind of standard?

T: No, I don't know what other medical school curriculum are, so I would have no comparison. Although you could, it would be an easy email to medical directors of other medical programmes. You could ask 'what do you guys offer?' and just do like a quick survey. It would be pretty easy.

MJ: Something to write down. I'm going to write that down.

Background

MJ: Tell me about your background and how that kind of led up to medical school and what you're doing now.

T: So, my dad is a physician, he was actually a surgeon and around the time [I was a child] he was learning laparoscopic surgery. And around that time, they would record them on VHS tape, and he would bring them home and that was my evening entertainment. Laparoscopic appendectomy and colectomies and things like that. I was around it a lot. He had me help. He would do weight loss surgeries, and so he would track the patients' weight loss after the surgery. And that was my job to track the weight loss on the graphs to show that the patients were losing weight as appropriate. So again, I was involved with that. He also had me volunteer at the hospital. So, when I went to college [and the question was asked] 'what do you want to do?', the choice seemed obvious. You know biology classes seemed to come easier and people gravitate to what they are good at and what is easier, and so that is how I kind of got into medicine. Then, medical school was in Cincinnati. I'm from Ohio. It's easier to go to medical school where you have in-state citizenship. So, I did Cincinnati, and then I went to Madison, Wisconsin for residency and fellowship. So medical school is four years, residency was 4, and fellowship turned out to be three – so another seven years.

MJ: *How did you choose your speciality [in gastroenterology]?*

T: So again, it's what comes easier. My dad had me watch videos of gall bladder procedures and intestines – he did intestine resections and things like that. It seemed to make more sense, plus there is a hands-on aspect to gastroenterology. It's procedure-heavy, so you do 70% procedures, 30% office-clinic consults – that sort of variety. Growing up playing sports, playing video games, hand-eye coordination, it all kind of gelled with this specialty. It's tough for me to tell my twelve-year-old he can't play video games because that is what I do all day. I mean if you look at it, I am staring at a screen and I am holding instruments with my hands: up down, left right. I have toys I can put through the scope, and that's what I do all day. Luckily, I am pretty good at it. You enjoy things you are good at.

The Patient Experience

With an insight into how Trip got into medicine, we proceeded to talk about his experience with his patients. Specifically, we delved into how hearing loss is diagnosed, how he interacts with people who are d/hh, how often he sees Deaf patients and what communicative strategies he employs in interacting with them, among other things:

MJ: *When you hear someone is Deaf what are your initial thoughts?*

T: I can't wait to use my sign language and say popcorn and do my name and try to use those things that I have tucked away, that's my first impression. Then I think about who's gonna interpret. Did they bring someone, is it their wife, is it their significant other, those are the first things that come to mind – how am I going to communicate?

MJ: *How will knowing that they are Deaf, how does that change your approach when planning for the visit?*

T: Oh, you want to make sure you are in front of them, right, with people who have hearing impairments. Sometimes they are so good that you don't need to sign, I mean there are people who are amazing at lip reading. So, as long as you are in front of them, they can usually – if you talk slowly, they can get what you said. They don't even say that I mumble because everyone else says I mumble. So anyway, that's the big thing, making sure you are right in front of them, who's going to interpret for them, who's going to help with the communication – and getting excited that I can use my sign language.

Recently we took care of [a deaf patient]. The procedure was a colonoscopy and the occasion was just for screening and cancer prevention by removing any precancerous growths. We see the patients in the preprocedural area, which is a room, so I walked in and I sat down in the chair in front of him. And his interpreter – which was not his wife – was next to me. We [the patient and I] actually shared getting to know you, 'Hi, how are you doing?' kind of things. Then I leave the room and the nurse comes in and gets the patient ready for the procedure, whether that's starting the IV, taking medical history, helping to get the patient changed. The nurse is there by themselves [no interpreter]. And after that the patient is brought to the procedure room where again I see the patient.

MJ: *The interpreter is . . . is that the right word?*

T: Yes. The interpreter is at the bedside until we start giving medication. And then once the sedation starts, they are asked to leave for the procedure. They can't be there for the procedure. Then we start giving medication, the patient drifts off to sleep through the procedure. Then afterwards, we come to talk to the patient to tell them the results waiting for them to be awake enough to hear the words. Some of the medications don't allow you to remember the words, but again this is a standard thing that we do for everybody. It is just involving the interpreter and positioning and where I am in front of them. That is the big difference.

MJ: *How did you get the interpreter, what was that process like?*

T: We can go out and if you wanted to, we could go out and ask the hospital because that's not done on my part.

MJ: *Oh, OK.*

T: So, there are things called *open access referrals*, which means that this is the first time that I met him – at the time of the procedure. Which means that a primary care doctor, somebody else, has referred him for the procedure and helped make whatever arrangements that were necessary. So, we can call, we can go out and see what the phone number is or who they contact to get the interpreter there on that day.

MJ: No worries, it's OK. I was just curious because you seemed surprised that there was an interpreter there.

T: 'Cause sometimes there is not. You know, we were trained that any time you need an interpreter, it should not be family, that's what we are trained to do. Does that always happen? No. Because the family member may not know medical jargon, may not be able to translate what I am saying into something they can understand. So, you really shouldn't have a family member as the interpreter. Maybe you can [hire a formal interpreter] in an academic situation, but for rural or community practice, it doesn't always [work]. You take what you can get.

We would like to have [a formal interpreter] but again, if I haven't had any chance to arrange it ... you know, you are relying on the referring doctor to make all the necessary arrangements, and that may or may not happen.

MJ: How often do you come across somebody who is deaf?

T: Probably about once a month, so I mean it's like eight to ten times a year. So, it's not infrequent. A lot more patients are hearing impaired than Deaf and so [in that situation] they can read lips, or you can yell, you know. There are ways to get around it. But for patients who are deaf – completely deaf, where they can't hear – then probably [I see them] around six to eight times a year. So, it's not all the time, but it's enough.

MJ: What happens if someone who was Deaf came into your office without an interpreter or anyone to assist with communication?

T: So, I haven't come across that. They are usually with somebody, whether that was a family member or an interpreter that can help. I haven't come across a situation with a Deaf person. Now language barriers sometimes ... They'll be the only one there – the patient. There's nobody else with them and then you are really stuck because you can't communicate, and they can't relay to you what their problem is, and you can't get any information from them. So that's kind of a useless appointment. And sometimes it needs to be rescheduled.

MJ: Until you can get the resources?

T: Yeah. If I see them the first time and there is an issue with communication, then on subsequent visits we will make sure there is an interpreter available. It's usually the first visit that shows us what we aren't prepared for. If we don't know if they're referred in, then we don't know. We may end up setting up the appointment with the wife or significant other and then the patient shows up and we didn't know [they were Deaf]. But if there are follow-up visits, then we're aware of it and we can [hire an interpreter] for sure.

MJ: So, when you are working, say with the deaf patient you described earlier, how do you feel about the communication between you and the patient?

T: I thought that everything that I wanted to get across got across. For me, I essentially communicated everything, and we had the interpreter and they were able to communicate.

MJ: *I am going to turn it around and ask how do you feel the patient felt with the experience with using the interpreter?*

T: I thought my initial introduction, you know, the saying of my name in sign language [was good]. It got a smile.

MJ: *How do you interpret what he is feeling or doing?*

T: Well he had a smile on his face. We had a back and forth regarding me catching his question about the two Ts versus the one T. So, I felt like right off the bat we were on a good start. Then the procedure and the rest of the day went as a typical patient interaction. So, I thought that it went well . . . and I haven't heard anything negative afterwards. [*Chuckles*] That is always good, no news is sometimes good news. Yeah, I thought the exchange, the visit, was successful from and for both parties.

The next section examines post-treatment communication with patients, specific communication aids, and communication services provided by hospitals and made available to physicians and their clients.

Outreach Communication

MJ: *I know you were the referring doctor, but do you do any reaching out to the patient afterwards?*

T: I do, so if there's a specimen obtained biopsy or polyp taken off, things like that, I will send a letter to them by mail saying what the results are. I would call them if it was something concerning. So that's with any biopsy results. For any procedure, we have the protocol of calling the patient the next day to make sure they are doing OK. Somebody here, if the procedure was in the hospital, probably one of the nurses would make the call. Usually there's a stack of call back papers that the nurses go through and try to reach out to them. Now if the phone number doesn't work, if the patient doesn't answer the phone, we don't get to communicate with everybody, but we try on everybody, the day after to make sure they did OK and if they had any questions or concerns or anything like that.

MJ: *Have you ever heard that someone called a deaf patient and ended up being an interpreter?*

T: Right.

MJ: *Have you ever experienced that?*

T: No. What would be interesting is if we could track them, I'm gonna see if we can track the paper because it would be interesting to see what happened.

In the next subsection, I offer details about the specific communication aids and services provided by the hospital where Trip works. As was made known in the interview, Trip is unfamiliar with the process of hiring or setting up communication services. Therefore, he invited a nurse into the small observation room, where we still sat. This conversation enlightened me in relation to the hospital's procedure regarding the follow-up contacts with Deaf patients and led to an additional conversation with another colleague who was familiar with the computer interpreting system – VRS. The verbatim interaction between Trip and the nurse is given below:

TRIP: So, I don't know what happened with the call back.
NURSE: With the follow-up.
T: [*Addressing MJ*] She actually, I think, may have made the call back to that patient.
N: I did. It did say on the follow-up sheet that the patient was deaf, so I knew right away. Do you know [*addressing MJ*], are you familiar with relay calls?
T: Yes, an interpreter on the line to help with communication.
N: That's what it was, and so when I called, the person that I spoke with said 'OK' and they then basically contact the patient and the patient is either able to read it or they are able to sign depending on which [communication device] they have. They didn't tell me which one it was. But the person I spoke with, I was able to say what I needed to say. She then communicated it to the deaf person, who then answered my questions. He was able to ask questions and I was able to ask him questions. We were able to completely communicate to make sure we knew how his post-op was, how he did, how he felt, if he had any complications, if he needed to have, you know, medical attention, which he hadn't. Everything had gone well. And that was about it. Then we're able to go until I can say 'does he have any questions does he feel good about it [*the nurse is addressing the interpreter not the patient*]? If not, please call Trip's office'. Then until he could say in the positive that yes, everything is great and that he understood the directions, that is what we would do. Then that's when you make sure that the call is complete, that the parties are happy with it and that's when the relay then hangs up.
T: Very nice.
N: Yeah.
T: Thank you so much.

After she finished, Trip needed to make a call and I was escorted by the nurse to her station to ask one of her colleagues about scheduling interpreters. It became clear that the VRS was used for interpreters in the hospital if they were the ones to provide the interpreter. The patient discussed in the 'Patient Experience' section of this narrative was provided with an interpreter, courtesy of the referring doctor; therefore, they were physically at the appointment. The first nurse then took me to the registration desk where they keep the VRS and showed me the monitor. It was a computer on a cart that could be accessed by anyone at the hospital. It provides video interpreting for many different languages, including Mandarin and ASL.

Trip then spoke to me about improvements in patient–client interaction as a result of improved technology:

T: Nowadays for language barriers in particular, they'll have computer monitors where you can get access to any translator you need. The university health system has a deal with a company to provide this service. I don't know if they have that for sign language, but they do for any language that needs interpretation. So, you would talk to the patient like this [gestures to how MJ and himself are communicating face to face] and then they would look to this monitor which would be a human. They would communicate in that way [for the entire visit]. It's on wheels, so you can bring it to any room in the hospital or anywhere. That is one thing that has shown an improvement in [patient care] training. It was in its infancy not so good, but now it is pretty easy.

MJ: Is the monitor system offered in the office in addition to the hospital?

T: So, the office is not, but it could be. We have computers on rolling tables in the office, we just haven't made it a higher priority to teach them how to access that. Usually the patient comes with somebody that can interpret. I run into more of the family member interpreter in the office than I do for a procedure in the hospital. In the hospital it's typically a formal interpreter as opposed to a family interpreter. In the office it's the other way around.

And it's just better patient care, I mean there's no lack of communication, it's completely fluent being able to say what you want and have them understand it. It may not necessarily be about patient satisfaction. For me it's not feeling like I've not conveyed my message very well when I don't have the resources I need in this respect. If you can't convey your message you don't feel like you're being understood, and you don't feel like you are on the same page. That's because if you are making decisions with the patient about the next steps, then you don't feel like you guys are on the same page, you know it's not best practice.

Conclusion

Based on Trip's final thoughts, effective communication is a requirement to ensure that the highest quality of health services can be provided. It is not just about patient satisfaction, but about fostering an environment, and a relationship between the patient and the provider that enables health and wellbeing to be the ultimate goal.

In sum, at the beginning of the interview, Trip greeted me with enthusiasm. As far as I could tell, he was excited to talk about a topic he rarely thinks about, not because it was unimportant, but, as I learned from this interview, because an encounter with a Deaf patient was rather rare. Indeed, such an encounter was not a topic of discussion between colleagues. But still, Trip showed a sparkle in his eye as he described his experience and his effort to make a Deaf patient feel welcome. It became my pleasure to listen and observe him as his story unfolded. I am now even more encouraged to continue my research in the area of patient–provider interactions, effective communication and Deaf experiences well after the publication of this book.

Living with Deafness: A Patient's Experience

Introduction

In this section, I attempt to address each reader directly because I consider them uniquely important in this communicative process. Without an audience, communication is incomplete. In particular, I appreciate my readers' (your) interest in the story that I share with you; a story that is not often told but is more infuriatingly overlooked. Everyone has a story; in fact, it is one of billions of unfolding personal narratives, as well as those personal narratives that have already been made known or have become widespread. We believe, as storytellers, as researchers and as ordinary human beings, that from each voice comes a chance to understand a tiny bit more of the massive universe in which we live and for that I appreciate every reader; a listening-ear, so to speak.

In the previous section, we encountered Trip, a smart and compassionate gastroenterologist hoping to deliver the best healthcare to all his patients, including those who are Deaf or hard of hearing. In this section, I will take you down another path – this time, looking through the eyes of the Deaf patient.

Adam, the interviewee in this section, is a spunky, kind and tattooed man who, despite a rocky start to his career, had fallen in love with teaching. 'Hello, how are you?', he asks his students as they file into the classroom each morning. If a student feels confident, they might respond: 'Good; you?' They may then engage in more than the interactional routine and follow the above-mentioned response with 'I'm tired', before shuffling to their desk. If the reciprocated greeting occurred, Adam beams and follows up with an honest reply and typically something about the weather or his drive to school. Another student may then join and a 'Good morning' is offered and repeated until the start of class.

Adam is a professor of ASL; in fact, that is how we met. I wanted to improve my sign language and his class was the perfect fit. Adam was my first Deaf instructor – it was astounding what a positive impact this had regarding my knowledge of ASL and Deaf culture. The class was no longer about learning vocabulary, but about conversation and understanding another world; just like any other well-taught foreign-language class. Adam showed me a piece of the Deaf experience I had been blind to, and, as I had been compelled/drawn to learn more about Trip's story, I was eager to hear about Adam's story.

To be honest, I was a little nervous asking Adam if he would be willing to share his story. He was very warm and open in class, but talking about healthcare is personal. I was almost certain he would be willing to meet and chat with me about his experiences, but to have them published in a book was a barrier I had not quite figured out, not to mention also needing to have an interpreter available for the interview. However, despite the apprehension felt by both of us, he and I worked together to make this research project possible. I was able to explain the purpose of narrative writing and affirm his anonymity, and he, in addition to being generous with his time, helped to find an interpreter.

So, on the day of the interview, I had my recorder ready and met Adam in his medium-sized office, with just enough space for a desk and three chairs. I was a little early, so the interpreter had not arrived, giving Adam and me a chance to catch up. This interaction in ASL, regardless of my intermediate competency status, eased nerves all round. As we were finishing our chat about his brand-new deck that he just built, the interpreter joined the space. We sat in a triangle, me facing Adam and with the interpreter slightly to the side but angled a little more towards Adam. This made sense since Adam needed to have a clear view of her hands, while I did not need to look at her to receive the message; in fact, it was important for me to look at Adam!

For anyone who has not used an interpreter, there is quite a learning curve involved. I was not an interpreter virgin before this interview and yet I still felt a little anxious. I had preconceived notions about the communicative event and struggled to find my groove. For example, I thought that there would be a lot of lag during the interaction. Adam agreed to be interviewed for 30 minutes and, because of my ignorant assumption, I was concerned we would barely have 20 minutes of conversation. It turned out that I was wrong. There was very little delay time and we were able to have a rich discussion about his experience as a Deaf person. This was just one humbling lesson I learned.

Another challenging aspect of using an interpreter was my inability to focus on Adam's individual signs. My experience with Deaf communication is that when using an interpreter, it is respectful and very important etiquette to look at the person you are speaking with, *not* the interpreter. The interpreter is only there to relay the story in your language; the *voice* is not theirs. As a hearing person, we are accustomed to respond to a sound, so it is difficult to break the habit of turning towards the interpreter when they speak. But with practice, it becomes easier to imagine the voice coming from the signer and therefore easier to stay focused on their bright and detailed expressions.

At the time the interview took place, I was enrolled in a college class, ASL 2. This meant I could understand many of Adam's individual signs, but often not entire sentences. It took me about 10 minutes to figure out how to stay attentive to Adam's expressions and provide nonverbal feedback while listening to the interpreter who was a few seconds behind. Even though I had the recorder, it was important for me to listen to the interpreter so that I could pick up on important details in case I wanted to ask follow-up questions.

Despite my lack of grace at the beginning of the conversation, it was a wonderful interview to conduct. I definitely felt more comfortable asking questions in this interview than the first one with Trip. I had gained more confidence, got to know Adam better and thus had a better understanding of how that unique interview ought to be conducted or managed. I enjoyed listening to Adam's experiences and thoughts on healthcare delivery. He told me a story that touched on one's lifespan development, provided examples of positive and negative interactions with healthcare providers, and offered suggestions for a more equitable healthcare system. Although his narrative interview is recorded in written form here, I hope readers can visualize the story in real time being told by Adam.

Before I begin the story, I want to provide a caveat. This narrative is based on the transcript from the interview. Since Adam used ASL, the transcript was an interpreted version of what he was saying. ASL is a unique language that relies on visuals and its own grammar system. Therefore, a translation into English approximates his original meaning. Even though the interpreter was well trained – a professional with the university who most likely provided a clear and accurate interpretation – crucial details, especially those expressed nonverbally, could have been lost during translation.

The Story

ADAM: I remember the first time I had an appointment with a doctor, and they were shocked that I was deaf. He [the doctor] was like: 'Uhh mmm, OK I'm not sure what to do, how do we communicate here? Can you read lips?'

Of course, most doctors use this huge terminology and I'll say, 'OK you're gonna have to write this down because I'm not able to read that'. Doctors hate that, they tend to have lousy penmanship, Right?! And so, you get the paper, you can't read what that says . . . and it's like 'OK thank you very much'. But at that visit I said, 'yeah, I can read lips a bit, if you speak slowly'.

Only about 30% of speech sounds can be seen on the lips. The remaining 70% are made further back in the mouth, and those who lip-read must discern the rest of the sounds from facial expression and the context of the conversation. Lip-reading is a skill and, even for the most talented, it is a challenge, requiring a lot of concentration and some knowledge of the topic of conversation [Georgia Tech Research Institute 2007]. Therefore, even if the doctor spoke slowly, miscommunication and missed communication is not a surprise, especially if the health provider is using 'huge terminology'.

At the front desk, communication is a challenge too. They don't know that I'm Deaf; they don't know who I am, if I'm a new patient, especially. I might approach them and say, 'I'm here to see the doctor, I have an appointment'. And they begin speaking and so I motion then that I'm deaf and then I'll say, 'I made a phone call to request an appointment'. Immediately they'll just hand me the form with a bit of attitude. Maybe they never met a Deaf person. They're not sure what to do with a Deaf person; they're not sure how to communicate. So that's definitely challenging.

Now that was in the past. Once I moved to where I am now, I have a doctor that's just awesome. They will provide everything; at the front desk they are aware that I'm Deaf. They'll say, 'Oh sure here's paper.' They'll write back and forth with me. They will explain what needs to be done, 'every time you come to the office, you will need to do this this and that' and so forth, so it's terrific.

Nowadays, I see much more positive attitudes services being provided, much uh better, and so for many years Deaf people had to fight for their rights. Especially with the ADA [Americans with Disabilities Act]. I think people are becoming more and more aware, so services are being provided more.

Background

Education

MACKENZIE JONES: *I want to first just ask you about your education and schooling growing up.*

A: OK, I was born deaf to a hearing family, all hearing family. I'm the fourth, baby. My mother found out I was deaf and then took me for sign classes and my siblings began to learn to sign as well. I was mainstreamed ... in pre-school when I was two years old. The preschool I attended had seven to eight deaf students with one instructor who knew sign language, basically signed English.

Signed English is a visual representation of English. This means each sign matches an English word and it is usually presented in English word order: subject-verb-object. For example, the sentence 'The monkey climbs the tree' would be signed, MONKEY CLIMBS TREE – one sign for each word. This mode of communication works for some and is often taught and used by people whose first language is English, typically hearing people. However, this is not American Sign Language. ASL is not a signed representation of English. It is a unique language, with unique syntax and pragmatics (e.g. grammar and the practical use of language). In fact, it has very little in common with English [Rizer 2004]. Therefore, even if you know signs and can communicate using signed English, a conversation with someone who uses true ASL is quite challenging.

Let me explain. ASL visually tells a story using facial expressions, body language, eye gaze, mouth shapes, hand shapes, hand movements and fingerspelling. The order of signs sets the scene, often starting with the big picture and working its way to the details. Therefore, a person who uses ASL may sign the sentence 'the monkey climbs the tree' as follows: TREE BIG – then if the tree is close they may point at it – MONKEY BROWN SMALL – then with a hand shape that signifies animal (usually a peace sign with forefinger and middle finger bent in a claw), they may move this hand up their other arm, representing how the monkey climbed the tree. Tree, Monkey, Climb. Quite different from English.

A: From there we moved to another town and I attended an elementary school with about twenty to thirty [deaf] students. Again, it was a public school. And I continued there until seventh grade where I transferred to ISD, the Indiana School for the Deaf. I was there until graduation, so from seventh grade through my senior year.

For college, I went to Gallaudet University. I, of course, played around. I wasn't sure about my major ... I was in liberal arts, basically a general education. I began to think that I wanted to get into geography, I love the study of the 'Earth'! So, I transferred to a community college and began my studies. But then I decided to change [and] go into architecture. So, I joined a carpentry school at another [local community college]. I was planning to become an architect, but I was working full time as a carpenter and going to school. [My studies became a lot and I considered dropping out altogether], but a teacher really reminded me I should continue with school. So, I finally got through and graduated with a B.S. in construction management.

Employment

A: The problem with the job force was communication. I wanted to be a white hat, basically to coordinate crews on the job sites. But communication was an issue. So, I looked for some time. I sent out about thirty different resumes. I went to New York – Long Island, New York – because of job discrimination. Basically, they considered Deaf people a high risk.

Adam is saying that even though he was qualified to be a manager for a construction site, no one would hire him because he needed an interpreter to communicate. The company would not make the accommodation needed to allow him to communicate in a white hat position that would enable him to coordinate crews on job sites. They repeatedly said his hearing loss would put himself and others at risk. At risk of what? As Adam pointed out, this is job discrimination and could have been brought to civil court under the ADA:

> MJ: *Tell me about your feelings during that and how you worked through those feelings.*
>
> A: Really, I had a bit of mixed feelings. Part of me really wanted to be able to show them that Deaf people can do this. They can, you know, be a boss. At the same time, I had some fear regarding facing the real world – hearing people. I knew that I would have to do a great deal of fighting. I would have to fight to get an interpreter, I would have to fight for my rights regarding the Americans with Disabilities Act.
>
> When I was young, I didn't have a strong mind yet, basically. I was more passive at that time. I didn't want to really challenge anyone and so I really ended up just dropping it thinking 'it's not worth my time, it's a waste of my time'. I do in some ways wish I had been more of a fighter for my rights at that time.
>
> But that's when I shifted my focus to ASL.
>
> A friend pulled me into teaching American Sign Language and I really began to shift my focus there. Once I started, I just threw myself into it. I began teaching in the community for interpreters [who worked] in the community and so forth. And then after a couple years I felt like my bachelor's degree really wasn't enough. I wanted to do more learning, especially about ASL, linguistics, the foundations and so forth.
>
> So, I went [back] to Gallaudet University and completed my master's. Then I began teaching at a private college in a major city and was there for two to three years. I then transferred to the [public university] in town

and taught there for two-and-a-half years before finally beginning working [where I'm at now].

The Patient Experience

MJ: When you go to the doctor, how do you think they are thinking about you as someone who is Deaf?

A: I am trying to remember . . . now growing up when I would go to my family doctor, as a young man I remember the doctor, eh, not being certain how to deal with it. And my family really handled it pretty well. At one point they would say 'oh what a cute little deaf boy, come see me and I'll take care of you'. They also saw my siblings and so I think it [the doctor's perception] really depended on my parents. But yeah, they'd say 'oh little deaf boy, you're so cute, the doctor's going to give you a shot and then give you candy'.

MJ: How do you remember your mom or dad advocating for you in those situations?

A: My mother always would be sure that she had all of the information, all of the details. She knew what was wrong. And then once I went home, I would ask her what the doctor explained to her and she would go through that. She would say 'you have this [sickness], you need this particular medication, it [the medicine] is going to resolve the issue; it's going to take away the pain'. You know that type of situation. She would explain what had happened [during the visit], so that was nice . . . My mom was awesome!

MJ: What about your siblings, were they supportive, or how did they advocate for you?

A: Oh absolutely, they were all very supportive.

MJ: Thinking back to your education and schooling – mainly Deaf schools, correct?

A: Right.

MJ: Were you ever taught self-advocacy on any scale? Or on how to navigate a medical situation?

A: No, nothing at all. Nothing, and nothing specifically related to medical. I wished that we had had that. I feel like I could have understood getting out into the real world being prepared, but there was nothing like that, sadly. Well, there was a health centre at the Deaf school, but not everyone, ironically, who worked there knew how to sign. And so, they would motion, and they would say, 'OK you have to . . . [*mockingly Adam signed the nurse's bossy facial expressions and the jab pointing*]'. Basically, baby signs, they knew very little. I mean they did not communicate well.

MJ: Tell me about some challenges you have experienced as an adult going to see a health provider.

A: So, as a child, I don't feel like I really had any bad experiences, whereas I do have some friends who have had negative experiences when they were younger. But in terms of being on my own, there have been through some struggles, but mostly because of insurance . . . As a child, my father had good insurance, and even then, I sense that they would do anything for people who can afford [healthcare]. You know, rather than if you are just a walk in . . . But sometimes in my life I have lived on social security and I've worked part time, so no insurance. I found that to be a real struggle. And there is a stigma associated with those people basically.

MJ: Thank you for sharing that. What other challenges come to mind?

A: Well, the most significant challenge I had was at the front desk typically. As I said, they may not understand what I am trying to say. Like, I try to use my voice and they don't understand me. I end up writing and the language between us oftentimes seems like we're not comprehending one another. I fill out the form [they give me], whatever needs to be done. Always the first time, it seems like I got an attitude [from the staff]. Though, from that point forward it usually seems to get better.

MJ: Is there an experience that stands out in your mind, maybe with a doctor that you wanted to kind of walk me through? Maybe how they communicated with you and how you perceived them as respecting, or rather not respecting you as a patient?

A: I'm trying to remember . . . specifically, no. As I said, I had encountered some individuals with a bit of a negative attitude, especially regarding providing deaf services, having an interpreter, having paper ready, having the VRI[2] ready. Now of course, years ago there was no VRI, possibly in hospital setting, but not in a doctor's office. But even in the hospital [with a VRI] understanding Deaf people's needs, understanding what they require, you know, what types of needs are required to provide accommodations [is important].

MJ: How does your experience change between different health settings?

A: In terms of the doctor's office, a hospital setting, immediate care, is that what you mean?

MJ: Yeah, and the one that provides the interpreter is your main doctor in an office, right?

A: Yeah, and actually I just started last year, but they're providing everything. I was incredibly impressed with that. Then the immediate care clinic, if I were to go in and say that I have a problem, of course they give you the paperwork that they want you to fill it out. They say we'll call you and you can come in and see the doctor, and so they take care of things in that manner. So far, with my experience in immediate care, the people have been pretty good, the services have been pretty quick.

At the hospitals, I would say it varies. Now some hospitals are just horrible; their service is just horrendous. The doctors and the nurses don't respond immediately. Some hospitals, however, provide good services: they respond very quickly, they seem to be concerned about the patients. And I'm sure that applies not only to Deaf people but to hearing people as well. You [addressing MJ] would find that variation as well. I'm sure people [of all backgrounds] have the same experience.

MJ: *Definitely all over the board.*

A: Yeah, absolutely.

MJ: *When you do find yourself in a situation where you're writing and you're lip-reading – apparently not in your current health office, correct?' Cause they use interpreters?*

A: Right.

MJ: *So, in the past [before your time at the current health office], how did you navigate that situation? Did you ever feel that you didn't get enough information?*

A: Oh yeah, definitely. You know, what I've done in the past is leave it alone. I would say I was young and stupid. I didn't do research, I didn't ask 'what does this word mean?' I really didn't do that in the past. The interaction with the doctor would go like this: 'am I OK?', 'yep you're alright', 'OK', and then I would take off. And so really, you make many mistakes when you are young. You don't realize, especially, how important these things are.

So, I would typically struggle, you know, try to ask 'What does this mean? What does this word mean?' Sometimes the doctor would give me infantile words if you will. 'Oh, you got a heart problem' or 'Oh your breathing is OK'. Very minimal. I [didn't] care, you know, after that point I got the message, that is the most important thing.

Communication

MJ: *Tell me more about the communication with the health provider and how that typically goes for you.*

A: As I said, sometimes I'll try to read lips if that's not effective, we'll write back and forth. [But that's not the case anymore because at my current doctor's office] they've already arranged for an interpreter even without me having to request it. They say 'oh there's your interpreter sitting over there'. So I am thrilled that I meet the interpreter. The interpreter will come in with me to the doctor's appointment.

MJ: *Had you ever used an interpreter [for a doctor's appointment] in the past?*

A: I often have depended on my mom. Now personally I wouldn't want an interpreter because of my private life. I'm fairly personal. So, it would either be my mom or my ex-girlfriend who knew sign language. I asked one of them to go with me rather than having someone there that I didn't know. Or I would just go by myself basically and write back and forth.

MJ: What about VRS? Have you used that before?

A: I did have one experience and I can't remember exactly. But they said, 'We have VRI, the video remote interpreting'. I wanted to ask some questions and wanted to make sure they understand, so they brought the TV screen in. And we waited for some time. They tried to set everything up, they tried to get everything established. Wasted 15–20 minutes, so finally they had an interpreter that showed up on the screen. So, they gave me their interpreter number, you know they have to give me that, and so I had asked for a particular number and so forth.

Anyway, there was an issue and they said no we can't do that. So, we finally got it all straightened out. Um . . . and had an interpreter and the communication seemed to be OK. But I feel like that procedure is really not reliable. It is not an immediate service. You have technological issues. It takes a long time. There was a wrong code number. Ugh, you know they can carry misinformation if you will.

MJ: So last week I talked to a doctor that has occasionally worked with people who are Deaf. And he said at the hospital they use the VRS or VRI. . .

A: VRI.

MJ: VRI all the time and don't have interpreters at the hospital. What do you think of this? (. . .)

Earlier you said you would rather have a family member as an interpreter than a professional or qualified interpreter. Doctors are taught (maybe in one class, maybe one time in medical school) that it's really important they don't use family members. How would you explain that as someone who is Deaf and uses it [a family member], but the teachings/results are the opposite?

A: Right, and I understand that point of view. I think it really depends on the level of the illness. If it's a severe illness, if we're talking about cancer, if you are in severe health decline, it's not a good time to have family involved because of all the emotions. But if I am going to the doctor for a physical for a check-up, it really is fine if my mom comes in. You know, she's seen my private parts, I don't care. So normally I would say that's the case, if you are talking about the hospital and a serious situation, absolutely have a professional interpreter. Those are very different situations.

MJ: Thank you.

Health Provider Education

MJ: What would you suggest regarding training for health providers and their knowledge of working with people who are Deaf?

A: I would recommend that doctors take ASL classes. Yeah to me it's clear, take an ASL class. You are going to meet a wide variety of people. Even Spanish, take a Spanish class. You know you may have to have a Spanish interpreter . . . if you provide interpreters. At many hospitals I know they contract with specific agencies, maybe one or two agencies. If an emergency arises, they have someone to call.

So, in terms of education, I would say be sure that you learn how to communicate with Deaf people. Know the interpreting agencies in your area. Take an ASL class or two. Exposure to Deaf culture, I think, is important.

The following conversation arose when I asked Adam to expand on his comment about the importance of health providers being familiar with Deaf culture. Remember, we are speaking two very different languages. Even with a skilled interpreter, there is a chance of miscommunication, and this offers an example of this:

MJ: Could you expand on that? How might knowing about Deaf culture improve or change the way a health provider works with you?
A: Well that's a really good question. Obviously, it [*unsure what Adam is referencing*] is a great deal of work for a Deaf person. If you are talking about partnering together with individuals [Deaf people and health providers], maybe create a small committee to come up with different ideas: how we could best develop ways to help the medical community, how they could actually improve. Then maybe providing an in-service. You know calling the administrators, having a meeting with the doctors, with the nurses and so forth. Providing workshops, maybe one day special workshops. Something to that effect. Providing that information for them. I know actually getting started can be tough, but once you begin to do that, I think that you would see a great deal of awareness improve.

MJ: For you personally, how do you feel it would change your experience if your doctor understood Deaf culture?
A: Oh well wow . . . uhm yeah, I don't feel like it would influence me necessarily, except it would, maybe, create more of a connection [with the doctor]. But based on different experiences that I've had, I think it [understanding Deaf culture] could have more of an impact in terms of [knowing] what's lacking [as far as accommodations and effective communication within a healthcare setting]. Rather than being someone who's providing only what's needed, you tend to notice what's missing. Does that make sense?

MJ: So, clarifying, if the provider had more awareness of Deaf culture, they would see what was missing in the office in order to help you, rather than just

knowing what they should provide you? Is it about looking at you as an individual person, looking at your individual needs?
A: Well, that's a good point. I have never had a doctor that understood Deaf culture, so I really couldn't say. Currently, the doctor that I have, my new doctor, has just begun to learn about providing interpreters, about services and so forth and I am wondering how he's become aware of that information. He's always busy so I never have time to chat about it, but yeah that's a good question. You know the doctor actually asks me, as a client, as a customer, how are you? Are your needs being met? Are you satisfied with the interpreter? I have never seen anything in my life like this. Times have truly changed.

Note that even though the question I asked was not understood at first, if worked backwards, Adam pointed out the lack of cultural awareness among healthcare providers, the impact awareness can have on providing quality services, and how collaboration and community involvement could be one way to improve the delivery of health services.

Ending the Interview

MJ: *When you think about the whole healthcare system, what is one thing that you hope changes in the near future?*
A: OH, uhm [*rubs hands together vigorously thinking*]. Huh, better medicine for everyone! Ha-ha. But really, in general, an increasing understanding of Deaf culture. You know what, if there were one Deaf person working at each of these locations, that could be exposure to those who were providing services.
Also, providing better interpreting services, not just through VRI, but a qualified interpreter, that's a big goal. So: (1) interpreting services versus using VRI and looking at an interpreter who's highly qualified, and (2) also having individuals that work at the health centre and so forth who are aware of those important issues.

Concluding Thoughts

There is no doubt that these stories touch on our sympathies, empathies and, sometimes, our nerves, and call on us to reflect on them, especially on their impact on the studied participants. They call on us to act by passing them along to ears ready to listen and minds ready to act in order to help mitigate any hardship brought about for the participants. The stories call on us to empower the studied participants, and other victims in a similar situation, with a view to ensuring a better future for them – a future where a level playing field is the norm and real achievements are appropriately rewarded. There is no doubt that I felt compelled to improve the life of Adam and Trip; however, the most important lessons drawn from these stories is the information they provide us with regarding the participants' lived experiences and how society can make them better. Perhaps there is a different set of experiences held within or beyond these pages that they may wish to explore. No matter what one's vision, remember the words of Max Ehrmann (1952: 2), 'listen to others . . . they too have their story'.

Finally, Trip's and Adam's stories were written in parallel sequence. This means that the themes that emerged throughout the interviews (e.g. education, employment, healthcare access and communication) were presented in the same order for both Trip and Adam. The reason for writing the stories in a parallel sequence was to enable the reader to recognize similarities, differences and possible disparities more easily between them. As a researcher, I see myself as a mere pseudo-epicentre – one who relays stories from and to the studied participants. The advantage in this kind of interactional rendition is that by placing the stories side by side, the reader may notice that the voices that I amplify bring to light a dissonance between perspectives within the healthcare system, as well as a lack of equity for opportunity among people with differing abilities.

Mackenzie Jones currently lives in Helena, Montana. She is a health educator for the Montana Disability and Health Program at the State Department of Public Health and Human Services. As a health educator, she collaborates with Centers for Independent Living and Chronic Disease and Health Promotion Programs (e.g. diabetes prevention, tobacco cessation, worksite wellness) throughout Montana to increase opportunities for people with disabilities to be healthy. She earned a Bachelor of Science degree in Health Science and Communication Disorders from Truman State University in Kirksville, Missouri, and a Master of Public Health degree from Indiana University-Bloomington.

Notes

1. Video Relay Service (VRS) is used to provide an equivalent to telephone services for d/hh people. It is a public funded service that is used for a variety of communication needs and usually for two people in different locations.
2. Video Remote Interpreting (VRI) provides interpreting services for many languages, not just ASL (In Demand Interpreting 2018). It is primarily used in a clinical setting to foster effective communication between two people in the same room who speak different languages. The computer interpreting system described in Trip's interview is the VRI. This labelling error is common. The problem, of course, is financing, that is, business and politics. For example, using VRI helps to save money; however, it is not completely reliable and a lot of deaf people prefer to have a human interpreter present, as they feel it is easier to communicate with a real human being because the communication is clearer. The struggle with VRI is a common issue because the interpreter tends to be professionally challenged sometimes, that is may not have enough professional competence to interpret correctly. The VRI company needs to develop a higher level of medical interpreting. It is commonly mentioned by consumers that VRI's interpreters need to be more qualified.

References

Ehrmann, Max. 1952. *Desiderata: A Poem for a Way of Life*. New York: Crown Publishing Group.

Georgia Tech Research Institute. 2007. 'Deafness and Hard of Hearing Fact Sheet'. Retrieved 29 June 2018 from https://accessibility.gtri.gatech.edu/assistant/acc_info/factsheet_deaf_hoh.ph.

In Demand Interpreting. 2018. 'Video Remote Interpreting vs. Video Relay Service'. Retrieved on 28 June 2018. Retrieved 19 June 2018 from https://www.indemandinterpreting.com/asl/video-remote-interpreting-vs-video-relay-service.

Rizer, Sarah. L. 2004. 'American Sign Language Linguistics: A Few Basics'. Retrieved 19 May 2020 from http://lifeprint.com/asl101/topics/linguistics2.htm.

US Department of Justice: Civil Rights Division. 2014. 'Effective Communication'. Retrieved 19 May 2020 from https://www.ada.gov/effective-comm.htm.

Chapter 4

NARRATIVES OF TWO IMMIGRANT WOMEN ABOUT THEIR LIVED EXPERIENCES IN THE UNITED STATES

Dema Kittaneh

This chapter is divided into two sections. The first covers the narrative of two immigrant women with the pseudonyms Amy and Hama. In the first narrative, Amy, a fifty-year-old Jordanian banker now residing in the United States (as a US citizen), discusses how her immigration status impacted her health. She narrates how she went from being a banker in Jordan to becoming a housewife and mother of three when she emigrated to the United States. From her narrative, we discover how her new status as a homemaker negatively impacted the physical, mental, social, financial and spiritual dimensions of her health. Amy laments the extent to which people refrain from cooking and instead eat out at restaurants and fast food sellers, leading to numerous health problems. However, she praises Bloomington, Indiana for the presence of many good gyms, the YMCA, swimming pools, parks and things needed to maintain good physical health. She also talks about opportunities for her children to volunteer and thus keep busy. She notes, disappointingly, that she gained weight because after childbirth she developed the habit of eating, sitting and watching TV and eating fast food that eventually led to her being diagnosed as prediabetic. Her husband's health problems have included having heart problems, diabetes and high blood pressure, as well as being overweight, having high cholesterol and suffering two heart attacks. She wished that, like in Jordan, her neighbours and friends in the United States would complain about her weight as this could have helped her to keep it in check. She commends the Affordable Health Act (Obamacare) for making healthcare affordable to her and her family.

In the second narrative, Hama, an immigrant from Nigeria with five children aged 21, 19, 14, 11 and 4 months, narrates her experience of leaving Nigeria and settling in the United States. She brought her family to the United States because of her family's inability to live peacefully due to the terrorist group Boko Haram. Hama emigrated to the United States at the age of nineteen as a result of getting married and had lived in Bloomington for twenty-two years by the time the interview took place. She talks about her financial independence and the fact that for the first time in her life, she was able to work. She talks about the difficulties her husband encountered in his search for employment because of discrimination and how things have now changed for the better in Bloomington, thereby enabling her husband to find a job. It is the change in attitude towards Black people in Bloomington that has helped them to be financially healthy and has enabled them to pay for accommodation, health and food, as well as to save some of their money. Hama also praises the US healthcare system and compares it with the Nigerian healthcare system, which she says is nothing to write home about. On the subject of social health, she said her daughter initially had problems with wearing the hijab, but this was quickly solved when the child participated in a TV programme. Hama's spiritual health is different from her husband's because unlike her husband, who has American friends, she has only non-American friends.

The Story of Amy, a Jordanian Immigrant Living in the United States

Introduction

By 2017, immigration to the United States accounted for one-fifth of the total migration around the world (Batalova, Blizzard and Bolter 2018). According to the American Community Survey (ACS 2016) data, more than 43.7 million immigrants resided in the United States in 2016, accounting for 13.5% of the total US population of 323.1 million. Between 2015 and 2016, the foreign-born population in the United States increased by about 449,000, or 1%, a slower rate than the 2.1% growth experienced between 2014 and 2015. In 2017, immigrants and their US-born children numbered approximately 86.4 million, or 27% of the overall US population, according to the 2017 Current Population Survey (CPS 2016).

This increasing number of immigrants to the United States has its effects and challenges facing both the immigrants and mainstream US citizens. According to Garrett (2006), some of the challenges faced by immigrants include difficulties speaking and learning English, raising children and helping them succeed in school, securing work and housing, accessing social services, using transportation and overcoming cultural barriers.

Regarding perception towards immigration, Batalova, Blizzard and Bolter (2018) have noted that there is, on the one hand, a perception of immigration as a valuable source of human resources or human capital and, on the other hand, as a major challenge. Indeed, they rightly note that immigration is closely tied to discussions about the US national security, its economy and global competitiveness, and its role in humanitarian protection during this era of record global mass human movement.

As Aday (2001) has argued, immigrants constitute a vulnerable population being at an increased risk for poor physical, psychological, and social health outcomes and inadequate healthcare (see also Flaskerud and Winslow 1998). According to Derose, Escarce and Lurie (2007), immigrants' vulnerability is, in part, brought about by political and social marginalization and a lack of socioeconomic and societal resources. Derose, Escarce and Lurie (2007) further note that addressing the healthcare needs of immigrant populations is challenging due to the heterogeneity of immigrant populations, as well as to federal and state policies that restrict some immigrants' access to healthcare.

It is anticipated that through Amy's story, readers' eyes will be opened to the challenges that come from immigration and their impact on immigrants' health. Amy shares her unique experience with us and hopes for solutions via the enactment of appropriate public health policies.

As we learn from Amy, being an immigrant in the United States has its own challenges, especially when you come from a conservative culture like that of Jordan in the Middle East! Amy emigrated to the United States by pure coincidence. It all began when she was invited to attend the graduation party of her cousin.

Amy's transformation from being a beautiful independent woman working as a banker in Jordan to a housewife and a mother of three in the United States has had its effects on her different dimensions of health, namely, physical, mental, social, financial and spiritual. Her story provides the details of this journey and the transformation that came as a result. Amy is a beautiful middle-aged fifty-year-old woman. She is a woman with Middle Eastern features, a woman with a strong will, wisdom and a kind heart who loves to give and not receive. At the time of the interview, I had known her for eight months. She is lively, full of energy and likes to talk, interact and socialize with people.

The Story

AMY: I came for a visit in 1992 to Chicago; my uncle threw a big party for me to meet his niece, and it happened! I met my husband and we clicked, and within two months I got married and before one year we had our first child. It all happened, and I stayed in US. On July 2nd, it's going to be almost twenty-six years. I like it here, it's nice, especially Bloomington, I love it. You don't feel like it's so much different than back home, small community, small environment. You don't feel you are lost because it's a small town and safe for raising kids. I love this so much!

I ended up here because my husband came as a student to Indiana University-Bloomington (IU) in 1976 and didn't return home; he stayed in US and we stayed here. He had a small business and I just felt this was the right town to have and raise my kids here, and I like it so much. I don't like to drive for long or use highways! Everything is around you; the people are more open-minded, they are educated because of IU, there are so many international students and people of different ethnicities. So, people don't look different [at you] because they are used to this international idea from IU and I like it here so much.

DEMA KITTANEH: *How has living in Bloomington affected your kids' health in general?*

A: The health of my kids . . . The lifestyle is what matters, some people have lazy lifestyle that is going to affect them in the long run; for example, the way they cook, how they live at home. I don't think Bloomington as a town negatively affects your heath, it's your own lifestyle that affects your health. Whether you are active or not, whether or not you are lazy, or eat healthy foods, this is what accumulates problems. Bloomington as a town is nice, there are so many restaurants, but you don't have to eat there, you don't have to go out to eat!

DK: *How about their [your children's] physical health?*

A: Everything you want is here. If you want a gym, there is a gym; there are parks, swimming pools and everything around. Bloomington is a positive place to increase their physical activity. My kids had memberships in YMCA for the past eighteen years. I used to sign them up in so many programmes; it's a very nice environment for raising kids, they benefit so much from here. Their personality is different, they became more confident in themselves. They also learned how to live in a community and be part of it. They help in the community like real American citizens because they were born here, and I like how they are involved in the community. They were involved in many activities to help the community. For example, Habitat for Humanity, for helping old people, people with no homes and they helped in building houses. My youngest daughter is doing Riley

Hospital, Key Club, helping in the community doing these things. This is good for them, making them part of community and keeping them more confident in themselves. It makes them belong to Bloomington and USA. Because they don't know my country, they feel like strangers there! They don't know anybody, neither their own aunts nor uncles! Here their friends are their families, as if they are their brothers and sisters, because they have lived here much more than they have lived in my home country.

DK: *At what age did you move to the United States of America?*

A: I came here in 1992, I was twenty-three years old. I got my first daughter in 1993, my son in 1996 and my second daughter in 2000.

DK: *What kind of activities influenced your health? Activities coming from home, workplace or from school.*

A: After I came USA, I used to walk with my husband around the blocks. Bloomington streets have sidewalks. Then, I had my first pregnancy, I started gaining so much weight and the doctor recommended that I walk, after I had the baby, I gained more weight and didn't lose it.

DK: *Why did you gain more weight?*

A: Because I used to stay home most of the time doing nothing. My lifestyle was the lazy type that involved eating, sitting and watching TV. When I first came to the USA, there were lots of new things to try, we used to eat a lot outside, that made me gain weight because moving to USA is a new experience for me. The biggest problem was fast food, it affected me so much because with my busy schedule, I didn't have enough time to cook healthy meals for my family, so I started getting food from fast food restaurants. At the beginning it did not affect me, but after a while it affected me and the kids. We started gaining weight, being lazy, did not want to go anywhere and then lots of health problems started to appear at that time. I then realized that the weight I gained started affecting my health, so I tried to hold back on all those stuffs. It took me a long time before I realized it but finally, I did.

Another reason you don't get concerned about gaining weight in the US is because people here don't look at each other, and there is a big percentage of big people around you, so you feel normal. But back home everyone watches their weight and the weight of their friends and neighbours because they want to look good. In my country people look at each other a lot, so if you gain a little bit weight, they'll ask you why you have you gained weight. So, you feel there is always someone monitoring you and looking at you all the time, so you try to hold off from gaining weight, but here, I felt like everyone else. Nobody will ask you why you gained weight or why you are not trying to lose weight. I felt lost between people because there are a lot of people like me and worse, so I did not think I was bad.

This has a bad effect on you; you don't watch your weight, and you don't feel you are being watched and monitored by other people. It feels as if no one is on top of your head watching and warning you. You live your free life all the time. But I prefer my home-country style of controlling yourself, so you don't have to go through diet. So, the lifestyle back home is easier; here there is so much food around you. Money issue plays a big thing in my country because people can't afford eating outside as much as they do here in USA. The salaries here are better so people don't care about spending money here; if they don't have cash, they will use their credit card, so that make them have always money at hand. However, back home people are careful about what they spend and how much, they will spend on necessary stuff. It is considered luxury and a big celebration, to eat outside in Jordan, but here in the United States, it's not normal to eat at home, most people eat outside.

DK: Did anybody say anything when you went back to your home country?

A: Yeah . . . Everybody! It was like a shock to them, Oh my God, Amy!! What happened to you? You should come back! What happened to your beautiful body? What happened to you? Yeah, everyone started commenting on my weight gain! Criticizing me for that!

DK: How did that make you feel?

A: I felt bad because I changed! I didn't take care of myself. And at the same time, I felt good because people still remember me and like me the way I used to be. Of course, they still liked me even though I gained weight, but they preferred the old Amy. It's always good to remember the good old days!

DK: Did that influence you to lose weight?

A: Yes, it did. I did not lose weight just because of this; my biggest motivation was to be healthy and to get rid of my health problems.

DK: What positive thing did you gain from living in the USA?

A: This is the positive thing: new experience, new country and a new lifestyle. I had three children which is a positive thing that added to my life. But in the long run when you have to think about it, you have to be healthy and active to keep up with these kids. You have to take them here and there and take them around. You have to be active, not lazy, and I couldn't move, so I started looking after my weight and my lifestyle. I changed all these not just for my kids, but also because I suffered from health issues; I was diagnosed as prediabetic at an early age and this is not good.

DK: What other negative consequences other than becoming prediabetic did you suffer from?

A: Laziness, I felt so much tired, so much weight. I don't want to move around; I was not active. I always liked to just sit down doing nothing.

You felt like you are moving as two persons, not one! So, you feel much lazy!

DK: Can you list strategies that helped you deal with the health problems that influenced your health?

A: The first strategy was I cut off all these junk foods and junk places. I never ate outside anymore. I started cooking at home, healthy stuff, my traditional old cooking in a healthy way. I limited dining out to once every two to three weeks instead of going two to three times weekly. I started walking and taking the kids out for walking, to the parks and doing activities, and this helped me in getting back my energy, my old lifestyle. It helped me to lose so much weight and helped me to spend more time with the kids.

DK: Do you think being in the USA helped you in dealing with your weight gain?

A: It helped me through education. In the USA, the health system helps to educate you, to prevent the problem weight gain. Like, for example, back in my country, if the doctor saw you were gaining weight, he/she will tell you to lose weight, but you have to be on your own! But here in USA, your doctor will send you to educational programmes, to teach you how to lose weight in a professional way that is customized to your needs, not in a random way, so the process of losing weight will not affect you.

DK: Can you explain further how you were referred to a dietician?

A: It was my primary care doctor who discovered my health problems and referred me to a diabetic educational programme that taught me how to eat healthy, the correct proportions of different nutrients I needed to eat that fit my lifestyle, and activities that won't let me feel exhausted.

DK: Why did you go to see a doctor in the first place?

A: I used to have check-ups every three months and my blood results showed that I'm starting to be prediabetic, the doctor and I discussed it and she referred me to the dietician in the diabetic educational programme.

DK: Did you have insurance?

A: Yes

DK: Is it important to have insurance here in USA?

A: If I don't have insurance, you can't afford it; this kind of programmes are so expensive. To see a doctor here is not easy if you don't have insurance. The healthcare here is so expensive.

DK: What strategies helped you to deal with problems that influenced your health?

A: Eh . . . One of the strategies was to contact my doctor, get to see her and tell her what's going on. If I felt something new or strange in my body, we would talk about it and she would recommend what to do; she would refer me to what I was supposed to do whether to have lab work done, do exercise . . . do this, do that . . .

The main thing is that if I have any health issues, I contact my internal medicine doctor and right away and from there, she guides me and recommends what to do.

DK: *Any other strategies you came up with your own?*

A: I had two main health issues: gaining weight and my becoming prediabetic. I tried to go the healthy way through my own experience by controlling my eating habits, changing to healthy ways of eating, good choices, stuff like that. I have a list of ways I had to do to lose weight, I first had a dietician, I lost so much weight, but you get to a point where you stop, so it was frustrating for me so the doctor recommended stomach lap-band surgery. I did it, it was very nice, and I benefited so much from it; I lost almost 70 pounds. It was very good.

DK: *Did you have any complications?*

A: There is complication at the beginning of any kind of surgery, so this major one had its own unique complications.

DK: *When did you do it?*

A: I did it in 2016, two years ago.

DK: *Can you explain it?*

A: Took a deep breath (*sighs*) . . . They divide your stomach to two halves: the first pouch where you have the food then the ring, so the food will go to the first pouch slowly through the ring, as if you are having two stomachs! So, at the beginning because I was not used to eating slowly, I used to eat fast, so the food went up and I started vomiting and started getting dizzy sometimes, but with time and patience and doctors' directions, it went well.

DK: *How long did it take you to lose 70 pounds?*

A: It took me two years to lose this weight and it helped me. I'm not diabetic anymore, they took off all the diabetic medication.

DK: *What type of medication did you use to take?*

A: Glucophage for diabetes and other medications for controlling blood sugar, once a day before dinner time to block appetite and to help regulate insulin, but with the surgery I got more benefits. So, I'm not diabetic anymore, I did blood work to ensure I was staying safe and healthy. My blood sugar level used to be high (A1c 7–8) but now it's normal (A1c 4); it dropped! So, the doctors told me I don't need to take any kind of medication anymore, so it's been now three to four months like that. I'm just getting on track, trying to keep the weight off.

DK: *Do you do any extra activities to improve your health?*

A: Walking helped a lot, mostly walking, walking, walking. It helped in losing weight and keeping the weight off.

DK: Can you explain the steps of the surgery?
A: It takes a while. First thing, the doctor puts you under six months of special diet, protein diet. Every month they prepare your stomach, trying to decrease the amount of fat around your internal organs, especially stomach and liver. The doctors tell you in this six months you have to lose 20 pounds and if you don't lose it, then they won't do the surgery because they are going to tell whether or not you are determined to follow the surgery directions after, because if you don't follow the direction before the surgery, then they know you are not going to follow them after surgery.

The most important thing after the surgery is that if you don't follow the directions after the surgery, you are going to end up in the hospital suffering from critical condition and some people pass away from these complications. So, during these six months, they prepare you mentally, physically, and teach you how to control yourself, your appetite, the things around you and how to change your habits, your diet style, and to change the kind of food you eat; this is done before the surgery. After the surgery there are some kinds of foods that I had to give up totally because you are not allowed to eat them after the surgery is done. I had to stick to things after the lap-band surgery, maybe you never eaten it before, but this what you have to start with, especially after surgery, first thing, there is the protein diet which is the first thing you eat. Your drink lots of water and liquid; this is the most important thing for the caregivers because your stomach is not the same size as before.

They put me on so many kinds of vitamins, especially multivitamins, calcium, iron, otherwise I could have had deficiency in them. Indeed, it happened to me because I didn't take the vitamins as recommended by the physicians. I used to have stomach issue from vitamins, so sometimes I didn't take them in time, so I ended up with iron deficiency, but if you follow the directions like the doctor says you should, then you'll be OK. I recommend the surgery for people who are overweight, who feel that their lifestyle is miserable, and they feel like nothing they do will help them, or if they feel depressed always. So, I recommend it to anybody who can't lose the weight by just diet, it's good for health first and the second thing it changes your look for the future. One would be more confident in themselves, feel that nothing can stop you, you can do it, you have more energy, you can do anything else and you will not be tired because you'll have the energy to work, and you'll be happy. You could work without feeling tired or sick from working. You will be healthier with more energy. You see, it provides you with a brighter future. You don't feel you are just sitting in the corner doing nothing and that your life is not being beneficial to others. You will feel you are doing something useful.

DK: If you are asked to help people to improve their health, what will you do?

A: They must know their problem, because if you know your problem, then you'll look for a solution or recommend something. Some people don't have physical issues but mental issues, so maybe stress or overwork. They need know their problem, then one can guide them to solve the problem.

DK: *What do you think about the healthcare system in the United States and how do you compare it to that of your home country?*

A: The healthcare system here is very difficult to get through. You must have a private insurance, or you have to be so poor to get government health insurance; it's not opened for everybody. You have to work to get insurance through your workplace. When I first come here, I had difficulties. I stayed for around four years without health insurance. I couldn't get it through the government and at the same time I couldn't afford private insurance; this made my health deteriorate because I didn't see any doctors for like four years, the only insurance they gave me when I got pregnant, was temporary insurance, a private one, till I had my daughter, then I lost it. The same with my son, then after a while we got this Obamacare and we applied to it and it meets all people's needs so we don't pay much monthly premiums and I can see regular doctors. I take care of my health better. If I feel bad, I can see my doctor right away. It's so good to have health insurance here because it's so expensive to see private doctors here in the United States without insurance. It costs you a lot of money and not everybody can afford it.

DK: *How about the quality?*

A: Like, in Bloomington, all the doctors are very good. IU Health is one of the top healthcare providers in the State of Indiana. All the doctors work very nicely. There are good and professional doctors. Some you know don't give you much time to sit and talk, but in general, most of them are good doctors.

DK: *Did you ever encounter any problems being a minority?*

A: No, the doctors here treat everybody the same, this is what I like about Bloomington. They don't take sides because you are from outside or you have different insurance or that your insurance doesn't pay this much. They treat all people the same; this is why I like IU Health, because they have good doctors, all they care about is that they give patients the care and health benefits they need, they don't look at money!

Comparing insurance back at my home country, we used to have full coverage insurance because of my dad's position, he was a general manger at the airport, so I didn't feel any difference between here and there regarding insurance because I was covered all my life there and when I came here I just felt the difference in the first five years like I said before but since getting Obamacare, it's been now eight to nine years under

Obamacare. We are doing good and thank God we got it, because I used to have problem with private insurance companies, my husband is high-risk person so nobody insured him and if they want to insure him, they put heavy deductibles and now with Obamacare we don't have this problem, especially that my husband is overweight, he has high cholesterol, had two heart attacks, heart problems, diabetes, high blood pressure, so he has the whole nine yard[s]! We needed here a good insurance, and Obama Care has met our needs so far.

DK: *Tell me about your recent work.*

A: After my kids grew up, I felt they didn't need me as much as before and I felt like I had enough time to establish a private business, so we started a small business with my husband, a small grocery store, and now I spend most of my time there. I feel I'm creating something by practising my personal hobbies like cooking, catering, having fun with customers, socializing with friends, making lots of new friends, making lots of new things around me. I feel my life has changed so much after we opened this store; it's a small store but for me it's a big thing, I feel like my life changed from zero to ten. It developed my personality so much; I gained more confidence in myself and the most important thing is I get to practise my hobby cooking.

DK: *Did your new work affect your health, working from 10:30 AM to 7:30 PM?*

A: It's tiring to stand all day on your feet, it takes so much time of your day and I sometimes get back and leg pain, but at the end of the day when I see the progress, where I got to, and when I see the reviews and how people talk about the store and about how we treat them, I feel all the pain is gone. You know, I don't feel I'm doing nothing, I feel successful.

DK: *How about your other dimensions of health? How are they affected?*

A: Everything!! Physically it increased my body skills; now I'm moving more. I have more energy. Mentally, I feel like I do something useful, I meet so many people in different fields, different people from all over, students, kids and families. I help lots of people, especially students, I treat them as if they are my kids. I like them to eat healthy instead of junk food out, so I give them good recipes to cook at home instead of eating junk food. I give them good ingredients and they are happy about it and come back to our store to shop all the time.

In sum, Amy's story tells part of what an immigrant woman normally passes through on her daily journey or routine in the United States. Her story is typical of what some immigrants usually go through or suffer from, even though she could be seen as one of the few lucky immigrants who did not have to deal with 'real' suffering that usually confronts poor or less-educated immigrants. Her journey could be described as a success and is comparable to those immigrants who receive education or good job training and secure good jobs. It is my wish and hope that Amy's narrative will shine and/or focus a light on issues and challenges that immigrants face while trying to be successful in terms of their health and wealth. The health challenges she encountered and her initial problem of not having health insurance will guide public health professionals in advocating for health policies that can address immigrants' health issues. Being vulnerable as a group, immigrants face numerous challenges and it is anticipated that the above narrative echoes the problems they face and provides an insight into how those problems can be mitigated or fully addressed.

Living as a Woman and an Immigrant in the United States: Hama's Narrative

Introduction

The narrator in this section, Hama, is from Nigeria. She is a tall, strong, well-built woman with a charming personality who keeps smiling and greeting people whenever she meets them. I met her at a social gathering and learned afterwards that she had a leading role in her community, where she teaches women the true pronunciation of Quran verses, the holy book of Islam, a religion which she practises. After I met her several times and learned more about her loving and lovable personality, I asked her if she would like to tell me about her lived experiences as an immigrant woman living in the United States – in her case, as a naturalized US citizen – and she agreed. Her story is presented below without any changes to the content:

> DEMA KITTANEH: *Tell me a little about yourself.*
> HAMA: My name is Hama. I came from Nigeria; I came for marriage. My husband came before me. He has been here long time ago way before I joined him. He went back to Nigeria to marry me twenty-two years ago. I got married after high school; in fact, I didn't go to college. I have five kids: 21, 19, 14, 11 years and this little 4-month-old girl.
> My parents and family all are alive and all living in Nigeria. When I came to the USA, I came directly to Bloomington. I went back to Nigeria to try life there! Actually, we planned to move back to Nigeria for good and we stayed for six months in Nigeria. Indeed, we put our children in schools, and we settled, but after six months a 'war' called Boko Haram started there, a group of people said that Western education is haram which means 'sinful'. They messed up the country, so they fought every

Western culture or education, they started fighting with the government and the situation became very bad and the kids couldn't go to school. They got scared, because they were attacking mosques, schools, police stations, so many places – attacking and killing! We saw a lot. So, we decided to come back to the USA. We bought a house here in Bloomington.

Now our kids have grown, they don't know anything there (in my home country) . . . they all were born here, they grew up here. We try to teach them how life is like back home and to meet with their relatives, but that didn't happen. We try to go visit every two to three years to meet with our relatives, we take our kids with us. Now we don't talk about going back anymore. We settled here, we bought a house and it's better than keep going up and down, and since the kids have grown up, they have the choice to stay here.

DK: *How old were you when you came to the USA?*

H: I came here when I was nineteen years old, I graduated from high school, I never went to college.

DK: *Did you work here?*

H: I worked last year for the first time in my life, but after I got pregnant with my last child, I stopped working. I quit the job before nine months. I worked in RCA, the food court in IU [Indiana University-Bloomington]. I liked to be in the kitchen, helping the kitchen staff, making eggs, sandwiches and smoothies.

DK: *How has living in Bloomington affected your health?*

H: I didn't have any medical problems back in my home country and the same here, but what I noticed is that the medical services in USA is great in comparison to the medical system in my home country, especially for the kids.

DK: *Can you give me some examples for how the medical system here in the USA is better than back home?*

H: Back in my home country we have lots of mosquitos and malaria. If my kids got fever from malaria, we take them for the hospital, they give them injection, they give them injections for five days for the fever which I don't really like, it makes them sick. But here they never give them any injection just for fever!

Also, what I noticed back in my country was that the medicine for the children and the older people was the same. They don't have different medicines for different ages. They do have different ones for the babies, but after two years old it's all the same!

They also give medication anytime, for fever they give injection for headache. But here [in the USA] they don't give injection easily. That is why I don't like it there [in Nigeria].

Also, there they don't have qualified doctors in Nigeria; you should be very careful when you go to a hospital. So, anybody who goes to a nursing school and learn how to give injections can write you a prescription which is horrible. But here I believe they have a very good medical system, a strong system.

DK: *How about the access? Can you compare the access to medical services in Nigeria and USA?*

H: It's not really easy. If you feel that you really need to see a doctor, you have to find a private hospital to make sure that the hospital and the doctor are really good. You can't see any doctor because lots of the doctors mess up the people's lives sometimes! I had a cousin who needed to have a delivery of her baby; she went to see a doctor close to our neighbourhood and they tried to do . . . I don't know what or how they did . . . they messed her up until she got very sick. The baby was not yet ready to be born, but they tried to bring the baby . . . I don't know . . . I forgot . . . they made her very sick . . . so they had to take her to a public hospital. This one was private, even the private is very rough you know, sometimes they get money and say we'll open a hospital. The owner of the hospital can have any doctors he wants, any nurses . . . no strict rules. Also, my mother-in-law had to go to a hospital, a private one, and the doctor did not tell her that she had diabetes; he didn't even know she had diabetes until it got worse and worse, and we had to move her to another hospital. They just kept her there and gave her different prescriptions. So, since that time we advise people not to go and see that doctor. So, it's very difficult to get a good doctor; you have to search very carefully to find a very good doctor. They do have them [good doctors] but it's not easy, you have to be very careful when you want to see a good doctor.

DK: *How about your children's health?*

H: My daughter had separate teeth like so many kids back home, but they never did anything to correct it, but here, the dentist told my daughter that he can move her teeth and align them. She started orthodontics (braces) for two years ago and her teeth are amazing now, so I feel like WOW! But back home we don't have anything like that. Back home, they don't have that kind of check-up.

DK: *So, do you think if you were living in Nigeria, would you have fixed your daughter's teeth?*

H: No, because lots of kids are born like this and we considered it as normal thing to have this kind of teeth alignment, so we don't think it's a problem that needs fixing.

Even here I kind of hesitated and said: 'How come? How can you change these?' And when the doctor said he can do it, I said: 'OK we'll see!' And now after two years when she finished the treatment, I said: 'Wow! I never saw anything like this back home!'

DK: Where do you live in Nigeria, a city, suburban or a village?

H: We lived in the main city. My parents live in local governance, and my in-laws live in the main city, and this is why we live in the main city. The distance to go visit my parents is like the distance between Bloomington and Indianapolis.

DK: How about access to medical services here in USA? Can you describe it? Is it easy to see a qualified doctor when you need one?

H: Yeah, I feel I can go easily, and I know here they have to qualify as a doctor before they practise medicine. Whoever is a qualified doctor is very good, so I trust them.

DK: Do you have health insurance here in USA?

H: Yes, we have it.

DK: Did you have it from the beginning or did you go through a long process till you got it?

H: No, I had it from the early time I came here because my husband had it from his work, before even we got the USA citizenship. Then, when I became a citizen, I applied for a different kind of insurance. And it changed when I got pregnant; even if I don't have it through work, you get it automatically from the government. It's called HIP [Healthy Indiana Plan].

DK: Are you pleased with this insurance?

H: Yeah, it's perfect! It meets our needs.

DK: So, do you think that moving here to USA has benefited your health?

H: Yeah, because back home we don't have anything called insurance! No, there is no help from the government, you have to pay before you can have access to the healthcare system.

DK: Even for the public hospitals?

H: The public hospitals, you can go, and they write to you the prescription. The public healthcare system is really bad. Whenever you go to a public hospital, sometimes they even don't have enough place to put the patients, you have to wait! It's really bad, so you rather use your money in the private sector hospitals; and even the so-called private hospitals are not really good.

DK: What kind of activities influenced your health? Activities may come from home, workplace or from school.

H: I exercise from time to time; I walk.

DK: Do you think being in Bloomington helped you to walk or exercise more, if we want to compare it to your home country?

H: Oh yeah, here it's quieter. We walk a lot in Nigeria, but the hotness of the weather doesn't allow for easy walking. But sometimes you have to walk to get to places where you don't need a car, or it's not the usual way to go to by means of a car so you walk a lot, but here it helps because it's quieter and you find places to walk, you are on your own, nobody is bothering you.

DK: Do you think here in Bloomington it's safer to walk than in Nigeria?

H: In terms of safer place, I think Nigeria is considered safe, you walk around people, so I think around people it's safer than when you walk alone like here. However, because in this city you trust people, you feel nothing will happen to you. So that's why we feel comfortable to walk here in Bloomington. There are rules and people here abide by these rules, so it's safe to walk here too.

DK: Did your children encounter any negative 'influence' from their peers because they come from a different culture or country?

H: No! I did not face this, nor did my children! They did not have any bad influence or negative thing, otherwise we won't feel comfortable living and raising our kids here. If we had seen this or feel it especially, the kids, we wouldn't have stayed here no matter what, but we did not face any such thing that's why we live here.

DK: So emotionally your kids were not affected! How about socially?

H: No not even socially! Actually, my daughter because she wears hijab [headscarf] – she started wearing it when she was eleven years old – the kids were telling her to take off her hijab! They asked her: 'Why are you wearing it?' She started feeling awkward, but when she became popular and started to participate in an activity where she tells the weather every morning on the TV, everybody in the whole school could see her, and they started to know her with the hijab, so she become popular, and nobody told her anything about the hijab anymore. They even tried to help her wear it, when she plays sport and part of her hair shows they tell her so that she can cover it properly and fix it. And they always encourage her and tell her: 'Oh, we like your scarf; can you wear the one you wore last time?' So, she became encouraged to wear it and she liked it, and she became happy.

DK: From your own experience, how would you compare physical activities for children in Nigeria and the USA?

H: Mm ... Yeah, even though we just lived for only one year there [in Nigeria], but that time we couldn't tell because we did not really settle, so we didn't know the culture. I can't tell whether my kids would have engaged in such activities ... But the kids do a lot: swimming, running, basketball playing and other physical activities during school and after school. In the summer we put them in swimming lessons.

DK: Do you think living here in USA helped your kids to be engaged more in these activities more than if they were living in Nigeria, or would it be the same?

H: Yeah, a lot of difference ... a lot of difference. When my kids went to school there, the teachers asked them a lot of questions: 'Is that right?'

One of the teachers solved a math[s] problem and then turned to my son and asked him: 'Is that right?' Because the teachers didn't know much, because as I told you about doctors, the teachers are the same! Sometimes they are not qualified; sometimes if they finish high school education, they can become an elementary teacher, so it's not really a strong educational system. The teacher, if he has a connection with the manager, can do whatever he wants. Even if you are not qualified, you can become a teacher if you have the connection, so there is a lot of difference in education system between here [in the USA] and Nigeria. We put our kids in private schools there and they all got scholarships because they were all very good and were ranked first, so they got discount fees and studied for free. They do that to encourage students to get high grades.

The curricula in Nigeria is strong, the problem is the teachers are not qualified unless they come from . . . we have different parts, we have teachers come from southern Nigeria, they are very good in English, and the syllabus and studies and school system are in English, so the southern teachers speak English. In northern Nigeria we don't speak English, they have problem in understanding. But I feel that in Nigeria they have more subjects to study in Nigeria and it's a stricter studying system. There is no play or fun; they have discipline back home, the problem is that they don't understand English because the syllabus is in English, the students there face difficulties because they don't understand and speak English very well.

For example, I went to Arabic school back at my home country and I did not speak Arabic, so I had to memorize stuff because I could not understand it because they didn't teach the language first!

DK: *So, you have both Arabic and English schools; do you have Nigerian schools? I mean schools which teach subjects in Nigerian language?*

H: No, it's either Arabic (the syllabus come either from Egypt or Sudan) or English schools. But they put our language as a subject to study.

DK: *Can you talk about marriage life and culture?*

H: We have a different culture back home from the one here in the USA. The husband when he's married can stay with his wife for the first year, but then his life will become 'outside' the house with his friends. He leaves his wife with the children, neighbours and friends. So, they don't have attachment like how we have here, so a lot of things, the wife gets her own way and the husband get his own way. He only comes home when he wants to eat or during sleeping time; they don't do things together, so that's very different!

When we come here, men learn to stay with their families and help their wives with the children. I like that way, when we go home, they look at us like: why he is always with his wife and family? Why doesn't he hang out with friends? So, I think this is a positive thing we gained from living here in USA. Because you need help, you know! So, we're always together and we do everything together. The kids also are happy, they learn from both mom and dad, not like back home, so that is a lot of difference between there and here and a lot of benefit when you live all together, the marriage life I can tell is better here, even when both of you (husband and wife) come from the same country, you stay with your family; the women need help in the home.

DK: Did you face any difficulties in speaking or learning English when you first moved here?

H: Oh yeah, when I came here . . . you know we got our independence from England, so we knew some English words, so everything was in English of course, but when I came here, I found it's different English. But little by little I learned, and I never went to school here and when I first moved here, I didn't like to watch TV to learn English, so I had difficulty understanding people. But when I had kids and they started going to school, they speak a lot of English, so I learned a lot from them.

DK: What language do you speak at home?

H: It's called Hausa.

DK: Do you all speak in Hausa?

H: No, my husband and I do speak in Hausa, but my kids prefer to speak in English; they are not very good with Hausa, but we speak to them using it. But they can't speak it as perfectly as us; they are not fluent like native speakers.

DK: How about raising children and helping them succeed at school? Did you have any difficulties here?

H: No because my husband is really good. He went to school here, he went to college here, so he knows, when it comes to elementary and high school it's OK, but when it comes to college, he helped them a lot and he's very good at it. He helped them with the homework, and he gave them a lot of support, and he's lived here for more than forty years so he knows the culture, everything very well, so he's always watching them and helping them; he gives them a lot of support.

DK: Do you think that it's important for you to raise your children in a way to keep them attached to your culture?

H: To me the culture is not really important! It's more about religion. Sometimes I personally avoid some things in my culture, it doesn't work here so the culture is irrelevant here. If it doesn't get along with my religion, I try to avoid, whether here or there.

DK: So, do you think when you go to Nigeria, you'll face difficulties in adapting to their culture?

H: Yes! That's what happened when we went there. We tried so hard to stay as we are since we had changed. We didn't have to participate in their culture; it's kind of difficult. We got a lot of criticism, we were judged and accused of not liking people. They said we didn't want to be with people, but that did not bother us because the culture is not from the religion so we did not care, and people got used to us and left us alone . . . yeah, nothing to do.

DK: Did you face difficulties here when you came to adapt to American culture at the beginning?

H: Yeah, especially me, because my husband was fine when he came here. He quickly met with African Americans, so he met with them and the culture was kind of OK. But for me I didn't have any American friends, when I came here, I just met with Arabs, the Arabic culture is almost like my culture, so I just stayed with them. Still now it's still kind of difficult for me to get along with the American culture. My husband and the kids go along the American culture more than I do.

For example, back home we don't celebrate birthday parties and I try to avoid celebrating it with the children, but my husband always does it with them because he feels it's unfair, because all of their friends celebrate their birthdays and talk about it, so my husband secretly buys them cakes, ha-ha . . . he does everything, but from my side, I try not to remind them about my birthday, but they know from the calendar, they just do it whether I like it or not. And I always tell them I never say 'Happy Birthday' to anybody, so every time a birthday comes, they wait for me, they say 'Mom, do you know what day is today? Do you remember?' and I'll say, 'Yeah', then they'll say 'You don't say anything' and I'll say: 'I never say anything, but I pray for you, but I never say Happy Birthday!' And then when they say 'Happy Birthday', on my birthday, I say: 'Thank you, but I don't care, and I don't want any gifts.' The same thing goes to Mother's Day, I tell them: 'Don't write me any notes or bring cards.' So, regarding USA-Nigerian [Hausa] culture, they still have difficulties with me. Ha-ha, I know, not because I hate it, just that I don't like it.

DK: Did you have any difficulties in securing work?

H: Since I never worked in my life, so at that time, last year, when I started working, my husband encouraged me to work and see how the life of work is. I didn't have any difficulties. Because my husband always told me about work life, so I felt I knew everything, so I didn't have any difficulties and I started working with the students at IU in the kitchen which I know all about. I have children and I've been in the kitchen, so I didn't face any difficulty, it's very easy.

DK: Was it easy for you to get a job?

H: Yeah. When I applied, I didn't even plan to work right away, I thought it's going to take about a month, two months, three months . . . so

I applied and got a reply within two days and they told me to get started, so I faced no difficulties.

DK: Was it easy for your husband to secure a job when he first came here?

H: At that time, it was really difficult. They didn't get the job easily especially at that time; they had discrimination against Black people! So, at that time he faced difficulties in getting a job because he told me some stuff . . . he didn't get the job and he never also went to some other places at that time it was very difficult! Even the school is kind a little bit difficult, he had to stick with the Black people so at that time [1977] they had more difficulties and discrimination against them, but now it's much better. So, he did not have a good job! When he graduated, he did not get a good job, he only got jobs like cleaning or jobs that are not really good jobs.

DK: How about housing? How did he get a house?

H: When he came with a bunch of groups of people from Nigeria, they usually stay in the dorm for the first year, which is not difficult to get and then they moved to an apartment where he shared with a roommate, so he always stayed with people from Nigeria or African Americans.

When we got married, we lived in an apartment for one year, then I moved to a new apartment because there were lots of Arab people and I learned Arabic there. Then I moved when lots of the Arab people graduated after September 11 and went back to their countries, so I moved out . . . I did a lot of moving.

DK: When were you able to buy a house?

H: Just two years ago; we thought if we did not get a house, we'll keep moving up and down, so we decided to get settled and got a house and made the kids focus on their studies.

DK: Do you feel anything has changed since you came till now?

H: Yes, people now have more education. When I first came here, people always looked at us differently, but now it feels easy to go out and people don't look at us like strangers. They look us in a better way now. I feel a lot of better changes have happened now.

DK: Did you have any difficulties in transportation?

H: No because my husband had a car since I was with him.

DK: Did you find anybody from Nigeria here in Bloomington?

H: When I came here, I found nobody from Nigeria; by the time I came, they had all moved, which is a blessing because if I have people from my country who speak my language, I would not have learned any language like Arabic. So, that was a blessing to me, thank God. For the past year or two, only one family came from Nigeria; in fact, since I came here twenty years, no one has come from Nigeria. I struggle because of different people and different language, I survived, thank God. I don't have people with same language, but from the other side I have learned Arabic because I did not have people to speak my language, so this is a positive thing!

DK: *In general, are you satisfied with emigrating to the USA?*

H: Yeah, yeah . . . I miss home you know, I miss my parents, my big family, we were thirteen, now we are ten, five brothers and five sisters. When I came here, there was no way of communication easily and when you write a letter, it took two to three weeks. No telephones! But now, thank God it's better. I miss the food also.

First time I remember when I came here, it was the first time I'd travelled far away, I couldn't eat in the plane, I was hungry and so tired, I couldn't eat from restaurant outside, just anywhere. I didn't like the food here when I first came here, so when I arrived my husband tried to make me happy, so he ordered pizza, and the first time I see pizza I wanted actually to vomit! I never eat cheese so my husband thought he'd make me happy with the pizza and lots of topping and I feel like I cannot eat that I see the cheese and I get more angry and he got so worried and he said 'You know what, let's go shopping' and we went to Kroger, and I remember I saw salad and I said: 'Oh! I know that thing.' I saw potatoes, chicken, bread and rice. Since I know how to cook, now I mix them and cook a meal that I can eat, and I felt happy, so I rather cook by myself. He was so worried at first because I couldn't eat anything.

DK: *How about now? Do you eat American food?*

H: Oh yeah, I love it, especially pizza . . . I love it . . . I love American food. Anything now. We go to different restaurants on weekends to 'try' [taste] their food(s)!

DK: *Were you impressed by America when you first came?*

H: No, I kind was scared first time because I'd never come here. I never even knew any country called America, really! The first time I came here, I came in the summer, I saw people walking naked! Ha-ha, that bothered me more, I remember telling my husband when we go outside in the evening when he takes me around the campus, I see girls wearing [not decent clothes], naked to me! I got angry and told my husband: 'Why did you bring me to this area, change the way take me somewhere else!' I felt so angry with him and told him: 'That's why you are living in America? Seeing people naked . . . blah blah.' And he says: 'OK, let's go to another place.' He was so patient he knows I did not know these things and he tried to be patient with me, he took me to another place, and I saw the same thing! Everywhere I went, it was the same thing, so I told him: 'Let's go back home.'

DK: *Thank you so much for your time!*

Summary of the Narratives

From the above narratives, we learn that staying home and/or being a homemaker negatively impacted the immigrant women's lives, especially, the physical, mental, social, financial and spiritual dimensions of their health. We also discovered how social isolation as well as the absence of neighbour's comments about one's physical size and overall appearance negatively impacted Amy's (the Jordanian immigrant's) physical, emotional and social health.

On the subject of healthcare, both immigrants talked about easy access to healthcare and healthcare affordability in the United States as a result of Obamacare, and the fact that the healthcare system in the United States is much better than those of their home countries, which is something that gives them comfort knowing that if they fall sick, they will receive appropriate care.

On the topic of financial health, the Hama, Nigerian immigrant, spoke about improved financial health given her ability to (for the first time in her life) work and make some money, even if she worked for a brief period of time. She noted that she was, during that time, able to contribute towards the payment for accommodation and healthcare. Amy, the Jordanian immigrant, spoke about how establishing their own small family business helped to improve her social, emotional and financial health. She was able to go to work in their store, interact with other people, especially customers (something that was socially and emotionally good for her), and make money.

Even though mention is made briefly about bullying (of her daughter) and its negative impact on her children's emotional health, Hama discussed how her daughter's participation in a TV programme stopped the bullying. Thus, the negative emotional health situation was quickly resolved via an opportunity given by the community for her daughter to be part of the community's TV programming – a programme at her school.

Both immigrants spoke of the 'lazy' lifestyle in the United States as leading to bad physical health and highlighted how physical activity such as walking, going to the gym or to the parks, and swimming in the various swimming pools in Bloomington helped to improve their children's physical health. They both also spoke about cutting out junk food from their diet and eating home-cooked meals in order to stay healthy.

On the subject of mental health, Amy spoke about stress or overwork affecting people and called for the need for such people to accept the fact that they have a problem and then seek help.

Finally, in terms of discrimination, both immigrants noted that the healthcare system (hospitals, doctors, nurses, etc.) are impartial in assisting all people, especially immigrants. However, Hama complained of her husband initially being discriminated against in job offers and how this negatively impacted his financial and emotional health. Nevertheless, she noted that discrimination was no longer a problem.

Thus, from the narratives, we see the immigrants coming to the United States, experiencing new facets of life, negotiating through the 'hills and valleys' of life, creating space for themselves to operate in and from, and making things work for them.

Dema Kittaneh holds a Doctor of Dental Surgery (DDS) degree. She is a wife and a mother of three boys. She received her Master of Public Health (MPH) from Indiana University-Bloomington, seventeen years after attaining her professional degree in DDS. She was born in the United States but was raised in different countries. She now lives in Jeddah, Saudi Arabia. She is passionate about health, especially, oral health, maternal and children's health, and personal narratives of patients who seek health in various health domains. She was a 2018 recipient of the Donald J. Ludwig Fellowship.

References

Aday, Luu Aann. 2001. *At Risk in America: The Health and Health Care Needs of Vulnerable Populations in the United States*. San Francisco: Jossey-Bass.

American Community Survey (ACS). 2016. 'United States Census Bureau'. Retrieved 23 June 2018 from https://www.census.gov/acs/www/data/data-tables-and-tools/data-pro files/2016/.

Batalova, Jeanne, Brittany Blizzard and Jessica Bolter. 2018. 'Frequently Requested Statistics on Immigrants and Immigration in the United States', *Online Journal of the Migration Policy Institute*. Retrieved 21 May 2020 from https://www.migrationpolicy.org/article/frequently-requested-statistics-immigrants-and-immigration-united-states.

Current Population Survey (CPS). 2016. *United States Census Bureau*. Retrieved 21 June 2018 from ensus.gov/programs-surveys/decennial-census/2020-census/planning-managem ent/program-briefings/01292016.html.

Derose, Kathryn Pitkin, José J. Escarce and Nicole Lurie. 2007. 'Immigrants and Health Care: Sources of Vulnerability', *Health Affairs* 26(5): 1258–68. doi: 10.1377/hlthaff.26.5.1258.

Flaskerud Jacquelyn, and Betty Winslow. 1998. 'Conceptualizing Vulnerable Populations Health-Related Research', *Nursing Research* 47(2): 69–78.

Garrett, Katherine E. 2006. 'Living in America: Challenges Facing New Immigrants and Refugees', *Robert Wood Johnson Foundation*. Retrieved 18 June 2018 from: https://www.rwjf.org/en/library/research/2006/08/living-in-america.html.

Chapter 5

LIVING AS BLACK AND BROWN
Culture and Identity on Holistic Health

Kourtney Ayanna Dorqual Byrd

The object of this chapter is a presentation and an explication of the narratives of two minorities: an Afro-Caribbean and an African American. The first narrative is about how the Black identity of a graduate student impact her overall health. The narrator, an Afro-Caribbean woman, talks about problems that influenced her health. She also speaks about how activities like sleeping (having enough sleep), hanging out with friends, having personal time, and eating healthy food help to improve her health. She complains about American food not being spiritually fulfilling and causing her to have headaches and frustration, and hence negatively impacting her spiritual, emotional and physical health. In the second narrative, an African American graduate student talks about the amount of work, physical activity (including exercising) and the type of food needed to keep him healthy. He also speaks about how stressful tasks and physical inactivity negatively impact one's overall health. The activities needed to maintain appropriate mental and spiritual health (through therapists, maintaining sensible and healthy coping mechanisms, etc.) are also elucidated by the narrator. Prior to presenting the narratives, I present a brief literature about figures relating to the African American experience within the larger American system of education, followed by an elucidation of the Black Graduate Student Association of Indiana University-Bloomington, an association that supports African American graduate students.

Introduction

Black Americans face racial stressors in their daily lives and these stressors can negatively influence their physical and mental health, and potentially undermine positive attitudes about their racial identity (Clark et al. 1999) According to the US Commission on Civil Rights (2010), Black students constitute 13% of the total US undergraduate student population; however, approximately 20% of Black college graduates attend one of the Historically Black Colleges and Universities (HBCU). In 2012, there were 12 million 18-to-24-year olds enrolled in college in the US. Of those enrolled, 7.2 million were white, 2.4 million were Hispanic, 1.7 million were Black and 915,000 were Asian. More specifically, Indiana University-Bloomington (IUB) has over 8,500 graduate students. Assessing IUB graduate student demographics in 2018, 4,897 students were white, 2,453 are international, 513 are Asian American, 386 are African American and 374 are Hispanic/Latino. The above statistics point to a low percentage of Blacks in US graduate schools compared to other groups. This chapter focuses solely on the narratives of two Black graduate students: an Afro-Caribbean and an African American. It is anticipated that future research will explore the stories of Hispanic graduate students and those of other minority groups on the IUB campus. We begin our elucidation by briefly explicating the Black Graduate Student Association (BGSA) of IUB.

The Black Graduate Student Association

The BGSA is an organization at IUB dedicated to fostering and supporting the academic, professional, mental and social wellbeing of Black graduate and professional students. Given my familiarity with this organization, I had an opportunity to enter this intimate space for Black people and foster relationships with graduate and professional students. I sent a recruitment email out to the BGSA list serve and informed them about a study on Black graduate health using qualitative methods in doing research in public health. Over 30 Black graduate and professional students responded to my recruitment email. Even students who were no longer in Bloomington still responded to my email. I selected the first two respondents as participants in my study because they looked more ready to participate and showed considerable interest in the purpose of this study: that of using a narrative approach to understand what kind of life experiences influence their health and any potential information that will help improve community health. The eligibility requirements consisted of being aged eighteen or older and being willing to answer such questions as: 'What kind of activities influence your health (activities may come from home, workplace or from school)?', 'What strategies help you deal with any problems that influence your health?', 'What extra activities are you engaged in to improve your health?' and 'What piece of advice would you give to help people improve upon their health?'

Regarding methodology, I conducted two semi-structured interviews, with each interview taking place in a secure location to ensure confidentiality and protection of the narrators' anonymity. Each interview lasted 15–30 minutes. I took detailed notes while each interview occurred, and I recorded each interview on a secure audio recorder that was stored on a password-protected system. I transcribed the interviews and identified emerging themes via coding. I also relied on my memory of certain key ideas and constructs that each participant shared. The first interview was with an Afro-Caribbean female graduate student and the second was with an African American male graduate student; these are presented below:

The Story of an Afro-Caribbean Woman

The interview for this section, as noted above, was with an Afro-Caribbean, a thoughtful human being who I have grown to admire and respect. It was a very fulfilling discourse experience:

> KOURTNEY BYRD: *What kind of activities (home, work, and school) influence your health?*
> INTERVIEWEE 1: Sleeping. I don't know if sleeping is deemed as an activity. It seems more of a necessity. [*Long pause*] Yeah, I think sleeping . . . So right now, I am very tired, and I cannot be a 1000% because I am very tired. The lack of sleep influences my health. I think hanging out with community – I don't know if these are activities – but, like, hanging out with community influences my health.
> KB: *In what way?*
> INT-1: Like, I think like that can be both a positive and negative influence on my health because I identify as an introvert-extrovert. Sometimes I need to be around community; I'd like to be uplifted, to kind of get me out of the slump and to encourage me. And, sometimes I need isolation; and I need to, like, to hibernate. I am at a point in my life where, like, my health and wellness centred around me spending a lot time with myself because I am going through a transition, I'm about to graduate, so I need to focus on who I am and my future. So, right now, being around people is very taxing and it takes a lot of my energy and it's exhausting, and I just don't have the capacity to do that.

Another activity is eating; I think that eating influences my health. Eating is very, like . . . I work in residential life and I have a meal plan. So, what I have access to through my meal plan is not always what I want to eat. So, my mental and physical, I'm very aware of the connection between my body, my spirit and my mind. So, if I'm physically eating something that my mind does not want to eat, or my soul is not feeling, like, connected to this food that is influencing my output, you know, and how I am showing up in the world; that is, if I feel energized and if I don't feel energized. So, like, there's no fried chicken! You know! There's no Caribbean food. So those things are influencing my health, and eating is a part of it.

KB: *Could you expand more on this whole mind-body-soul connection and how the things you eat show up or manifest?*

INT-1: I have really bad migraines all the time, multiple times a day or a week. I feel that the food that I eat – that is, dining hall food – is not filling. So, I am eating meat; I am eating rice; I am eating protein and veggies. But like, spiritually, I don't feel filled as supposed to like if I . . . like, usually when that happens, I'm, like, OK [Int-1], you need to, like, I don't really have a kitchen because I live in a residence hall, so I share a kitchen with the residents. So, I'm like, you need to find time to cook something; you need to have a warm home-cooked meal. There is nothing like a home-cooked meal. It's not really about, like, oh, but I am eating a home-cooked meal, but it is about something that's warm and made with love and care. I can tell the energy that people put into my food.

KB: *Wow.*

INT-1: Sometimes you just miss home.

KB: *Right.*

INT-1: You know, I remember last semester, I had this thing where I literally would just have fried chicken and wine and waffles. It was not . . . That's not a quality meal, you know. There're no veggies, you know, it's missing a lot of things. But something about it just made me feel full. It was comforting. And it's only like how many sandwiches can you have; it's not a meal. I'm used to having meals. I feel like when I don't have . . . or like having cultural food that's like from my culture, having spicy food, having food that doesn't make me sick. I don't know what they put in this food, but my body is reacting badly to it.

KB: *Wow.*

INT-1: I'm getting a migraine and my body is responding. Whether it's like, I don't want the food and it's a mental trick that is happening or like my body is physically, like, no this is not good for you; don't eat that. Or, this food is really oily, don't eat that. But, like, this is the option. So then, I get a headache, it's impacting my body. When I have a headache, I have frustration. So, it's impacting my soul and my state of being, and like all of these things are being connected.

KB: Thank you for sharing that. You also mentioned 'spiritually not fulfilling', highlighting how our spiritual health impacts our physical health. Then, you mentioned the word 'energy'. I am not sure if people really understand. . .

INT-1: They don't.

KB: What is 'energy'?

INT-1: Yeah, I wonder like how this content exist[s] in the academy. Like energy, it is not quantifiable. You know. Like how do you quantify someone's energy? You know, that's why qualitative studies are so important because you can't measure that. But if I'm telling you I'm not well today, my energy feels off. That's still a valid statement because that's my narrative and that's my story. You know. But you can't say like, how do you measure someone's energy? You just know. You know the energy in the classroom felt off, I guess they called that climate.

KB: So, would you say, if your energy is off, that also impacts/influences your health?

INT-1: Yeah, energy. Definitely.

KB: Thank you. Anything else you would like to add about what kind of activities that may influence your health like from homework, place or school before we go to the next question?

INT-1: Hmmm. My job. I mean, I think it's like everything influences my health. Literally, everything. There's nothing that you don't do that doesn't influence your health . . . because if I believe that my mind, body and soul are connected, then everything that I do will impact my wellbeing because I believe in like the holistic and the whole self.

KB: Thank you for that. So, could you name some of the strategies that help you deal with any problem that influences your health. So, what are some strategies that you have that came to mind?

INT-1: Strategies are very difficult. Because I think [pause] it all depends on the time. Everything in my life is circumstantial. Health and wellness are not a quick fix. It is circumstantial. We never consider the environment. So, like my health and wellness in this political climate is [sic] going to be very different than my . . . I started my first year of grad school during an election year. My health and wellness were impacted by me going to school during an election year. So, those strategies, what I did last year does not work this year as I am searching for a job. It's just different things. But some of the strategies that I have: I go to counselling at the Center for Human Growth that is like very important.

KB: What's the name of the centre?

INT-1: Center for Human Growth.

KB: It that here [at IUB]?

INT-1: Yeah, it's here. They do a sliding scale for graduate students. For me, I feel like it's more of a safe and inviting space. They have more counsellor of colour. These counsellors are doctoral students. They're really good. This doesn't discredit them. I feel like it's not a large degree of separation.

KB: *So, it's safe. Is this offered through CAPS [Counseling and Psychological Services]?*

INT-1: No. This centre is focused on growth and holistic growth. It's just a different kind of focus. I would like to go into that and maybe that would be helpful to the study.

KB: *OK.*

INT-1: Yeah, I've been going there. I know a lot of graduate students of colour who go there. It's just a good place. And my peers actually did a study on the Center for Human Growth and CAPS. I think they did an observation. They looked at the environment. So, what about this environment just physically, not physically, but of the indicators of the environment are more inviting than CAPS. They determined that the Center for Human Growth maybe has more warm colours, they have posters in different languages, and identify affirming things. So, it's really an affirming place. I go to counselling [*pause*]. I try to cook every so often to, like, get things in me that are well and taste good.

KB: *How do you feel when you are cooking? Is cooking therapeutic for you?*

INT-1: No.

KB: *OK.*

INT-1: Cooking is . . . I love to bake. Baking is very therapeutic for me. My physical space is very important to me. That is one of my coping strategies. Just making sure that space is what it needs to be.

KB: *Could you elaborate? What is physical space?*

INT-1: My room that I have, it needs to meet my standards. I'll go into that in a little bit. But I don't have a kitchen; I just have a room and a bathroom. This kitchen is down the hallway. It is a community kitchen for all the residents. I live on the floor with residents. That is not my space. That space is often dirty, filthy and disgusting. Even when it's not dirty, that's not my space! That's not my kitchen. As opposed to when I had an apartment when I was back in the past. I had roommates, but that was OUR SPACE. I could take my time and I had everything I needed. I had a cabinet that belonged to me. It just felt more like home. So now, cooking is very stressful because I have to carry pots down the hallway and then bring it back and I don't really have a sink. So, it's very stressful and it's a lot just to make food. Just to do something that I really need to survive, honestly. But baking . . . I try to bake very seldom. I don't like cake. But I bake and give cake to my students and that's really helpful. With regards to my space, I am really big on aromatherapy. I have like candles and incense. I have body oils for the night-time and morning. I have skincare routines. Just things that give me habits are also very good to ground me. I started a gratitude journal. I try to go to sleep but that's been more a struggle. I LOVE binge-watching shows. I think that is really important just to do that. Also, I am an artist. I try to connect with art. I've been exploring different mediums outside of poetry. I bought spray paint the other day and I have some paint. I want to probably experiment with some other things just to kind of see different ways to express and release tension. These strategies shift, based on the climate and time.

KB: Do these strategies offer you a release?

INT-1: Yeah, they offer me a release sometimes. I think [*pause*] when I go back to comment about climate, these are all external things. Right?

KB: Uhm hm.

INT-1: So, I'm realizing that the strategies that I need right now is internal. So, I don't know how to describe that. But the strategy that I use now is just sitting with myself having honest conversations about where I am and how I'm feeling. So that gives me . . . The internal work gives me more release and the external things just kind of create an extra support.

KB: So, these strategies such as aromatherapy, skincare, habits, gratitude journal; these are strategies that help you deal with any problems that influence your health?

INT-1: Yeah.

KB: OK. That's amazing. These are beautiful. Thank you for sharing. So, we are going to move to the next question: do you do any extra activities to improve your health? This is kind of an overlap question. You name connecting with art because you're an artist. This may be a little redundant. But if you can think about . . . do you have any extra activities to improve your health?

INT-1: Yeah. I've been trying to . . . I don't do this. But I've been trying to go to the gym and yoga for, like, forever.

KB: OK.

INT-1: I try to do that. When my friends come, I like to take them to the lake because water and sun are things that rejuvenate me. Going to other shows. Doing things . . . so I went to the Black Joy Collective. Doing things and being in community that is refreshing and rejuvenating. Someone once said: 'Depression is the ability to not see joy, and community is the mirror of joy.' So, when you are in the presence of the community, you can see their joy and hopefully that will allow you to see it because depression is the ability to not see, so I try to hang out with community.

KB: Are you intentional about the people who you hang out with then?

INT-1: Yes, if your energy is not right, we can't. Or like, I know right now that I'm in a very isolated moment in my life, so like I can't be around people because I also don't want to put what I got on you and if you got . . . it's just not, it's just not going to match. There was something else I was thinking about. I couldn't remember . . . I travel a lot. I felt like there was something else [*pause*]. You said were there any other activities? I don't remember the last thing. Cleaning is also good [*pause*]. Yeah, I don't remember.

KB: So, cleaning. Is cleaning therapeutic for you?

INT-1: Yeah, it is. It was something else. It will come back to me.

KB: My other question asked to list these activities and we already listed the gym and yoga; do you go occasionally or try to go. . .?

INT-1: I haven't gone in two years. But in my mind, that would be really helpful. Oh, I remember now what I was going to say. I feel like this connect to the word 'health'. I, in 2018, made a declaration to go to the doctor. So, I think we have all of these quotes on, quote, 'self-care strategies and tactics', but no one ever actually considers just going to see a physician. I have a lot of . . . my body just . . . my mind, my body and soul are connected. So, my body reacts when it's stressed. Because of that, I need to go [to] the doctor. I keep having random allergic reactions. So, I go to the doctor. It seems like something that is a given. But health insurance is not a given. That co-pay is not a given. That's something I have to actively recognize. Like, OK self, just take care of yourself, you're going to go to the doctor because you are sick if you're not well.

KB: Good. So, the declaration that you actually declared verbally, or did you write it down and put it on you wall? So, when you say the word 'declaration', what does that look like for you?

INT-1: I have like . . . I came up with like . . . I won't call them 2018 goals because I don't like New Year's resolutions. But these are things that I identified. Self-work will continue on for life. I think self-work is an activity of health and wellness. I put sticky notes on my door, and these are the three things that I want to focus on right now. It may take the whole [of] 2018 or it may take the rest of my life. But these are three things that I want to focus on. One of them was centring my health and wellness. Thinking about my identity now, I think just being Black, being woman, being queer, being Afro-Caribbean, you come from places where your health and wellness is not your focus. Have you ever seen the movie *Roxanne Roxanne*?

KB: No.

INT-1: Go watch it. It's on Netflix. You have braces. She talks about being the only Black person in the hood who had braces. And my mother, not my mother but people will always tell someone's social class and their health and wellness by their teeth. Right? Because who can afford to go to the dentist. I went to the dentist at Indiana and I was like this was expensive! They did all kind of tests that I never had before because I had free health insurance in the past. So, I think with my identity that I hold, my mother will take me to the doctor, but she didn't go to the doctor. So, she really had to say: 'I had to make this a declaration. I'm going to change this habit; I'm going to break this cycle.' Black people are not informed about their health and their wellness. The thing about being Black in the academy, I have so much work to do that I had to leave . . . I came from the doctor this morning before I came here, and I had to leave. Because I have things to do. I have somewhere to be. I have papers to write. And, I have to work three times harder than others! So of course, I don't have time to see two hours at the allergist to figure [out] what's going on. So, I think, I had to make that declaration because being Black is, like, conditions our lives, and the conditions that are imposed on us, they don't allow for us to bring forth our health and wellness. So, it has to be a radical act. That's why self-care is so radical because our conditions don't allow for it. That's part of the identity coming in there.

KB: *I want to go back and make sure that I capture everything and understand. You said, as a Black, Caribbean woman, health was not something that was a priority, essentially?*

INT-1: I mean, my mother says: 'Do as I say and not as I do.' It was a verbal priority only. But there were many contradictions. There were many things that contradicted that.

KB: *OK.*

INT-1: She was not mirroring that behaviour. She is taking us to the doctor, but she was not mirroring that behaviour. Then, if you were sick, they are like, unless you are dying, you do not need to go the doctor. Like if you are sick, it's 'this too shall pass' or claiming remedies like 'you'll get over this, it's just a cold'. Then, you have conversations about my mother trying to get me braces because she knows that this is something that she couldn't afford. I think, like, it wasn't a priority for her, but it was a priority [for me], but there are many contradictions in life that didn't allow for that to be as easily accessed. Then my mother would say things like . . . I would complain about my co-pay that I have in Indiana because where I lived before, I did not have a co-pay. She'll be like, there is no price to your health and wellness. So, she is speaking this value of health and wellness but not acting it. But then I have these contradictions in life, that's not allowing me to live these values that she is speaking in me.

KB: *Basically, talking the talk, but not walking the walk. . .*

INT-1: Yeah. Then when I try to walk the walk, it's these conflicts of interest, I mean conflicting items on my schedule. I have this paper due, but I also was just at the hospital until 2 am in the morning. You know. I think faculty members think like you are sick and then you are not sick as if a switch that you can turn off and on. I cannot be unwell and show up to class and still perform as if I am well. I don't think they understand that because being BLACK you have to always be on! Even when you do not want to be on, you can't afford it. So, your mind is like even though you are sick, you are dying right now, you were just depressed at 8 AM this morning and you still going to show up in class at 10 o'clock and participate – that is part of not being well.

KB: Wow. You can be physically present, but mentally, emotionally and spiritually not even in the room.

INT-1: Yes, that's post-traumatic slave syndrome. Physically doing this work, out in these fields. But where is your mind? You're not there.

KB: You're not there. Wow. Thank you for that. And there is no price to health.

INT-1: Nothing. Whatever it costs, that your health and wellness, and you can't put a figure on it.

KB: But not acting on it.

INT-1: But encouraging you to . . .

KB: But not realizing how that impacts . . . Thank you. If you are asked to help people improve their health, what will you do?

INT-1: The first step is to get to know someone and figure out who they are. I would get to know people and meet them where they are. I would ask people what is their relationship to wellness? What is their relationship to their body? What are their life practices? How do your identities show up in your life? Do not assume that swimming is the best thing for a Black person because it may be running. Historically speaking, there is a reason why Blacks do not know how to swim due to slaves being forced on a ship on their voyage. Overall, a relationship must be established so that people will be willing to open up and answer these intrinsic thought-provoking questions. One cannot be well if one does not know one's self. But I leave you with this, if you want to be well, tell me what you are willing to sacrifice.

The Story of an African American Male Graduate Student

The narrative in this section, as noted earlier in this chapter, is by an African American male graduate student. He talks about things that impact his health, problems and challenges he encounters regarding the various dimensions of health, and strategies he employs to deal with such challenges. The interview is presented below:

KOURTNEY BYRD: *Good morning. Today is April 7th and it's 12:38 PM. How are you today?*

INTERVIEWEE 2: I am well. How are you?

KB: *Good. Thank you again for your participation in this study, I am studying public health using qualitative methods. I'm examining narratives through interviewing!*

INT-2: Of course.

KB: *I just want to let you know that this study is a confidential, IRB [Institutional Review Board]-protected study.*

INT-2: Awesome!

KB: *I will refer to you as Interviewee 2. Do you have any questions?*

INT-2: I do not.

KB: *OK, let's go ahead and get started. What kind of activities influence your health? Activities from home, work and school.*

INT-2: When you say 'health', are you talking about mental health, physical health, or . . .?

KB: *That's a great question. What kind of activities influence your health? If you want to start off how you define health and then activities that influence your health.*

INT-2: Health for me is equilibrium. How balance is everything and whether you are effectively meeting your needs. I think of health being mental health, physical health, and health, of course, being connected to wellbeing. I think of health as being in a state of wellness where everything is in proper alignment and function. For if we know that appropriate blood pressure is 120/80, I think of that as being healthy and making sure that you are in those appropriate ranges.

KB: *OK.*

INT-2: So as far as activities that influence my health are maintaining balance, I think also the amount of work one has to do. The amount of physical activity, the ability, the capacity to do exercise and to eat right and to do those things. I think a lot of times, we think of those as things that everybody has the ability to do, when in many cases they are luxuries.

KB: *Uhm hmm [nonverbal sounds].*

INT-2: Do you have the luxury of free time to work out? Do you have expendable, disposable income to have a gym membership? Do you have enough money to purchase health food options? Do you not live in a food desert? I think those are the type of factors that affect it. As far as activities, I think of the way that work is done. If majority of it is spent sitting, then of course you are not going to get a lot of physical activity. If you have a very intense stressful job or graduate school or undergraduate school, I think of those activities significantly, in many cases, negatively impact physical and mental and wellbeing as well.

KB: *OK. Since you are in graduate school, the activities that influence your health will be, like, the amount of work, the capacity, to eat right . . .*

INT-2: Um hmm.

KB: OK. Is that pretty much?

INT-2: Um hmm.

KB: OK. Also, some activities such as maintaining balance also influence your health.

INT-2: Um hmm.

KB: Maintaining balance, does that influence your health positively or negatively?

INT-2: I think it can be both.

KB: Both, OK.

INT-2: The lack of balance, the balance making sure that you are juggling everything enough to make sure that you are getting enough sleep

KB: OK.

INT-2: That you maintain the appropriate balance between work and being off work. That you have an appropriate time management scheme. All those things I think about as far as balance.

KB: OK, thank you. So, list some strategies that help you deal with any problems that influence your health.

INT-2: I think about talking to people. So, making sure that identifying those folks who fall within my definition of health and wellbeing. Talking to them and finding out what that looks like, how did they manage to be healthy and even finding out if they are healthy.

KB: Hmm.

INT-2: Because the appearance of health is different from actually being healthy. I think about going to a dietician, working out, managing time and stress well. Bringing in . . . I go see a mental health therapist. Within that, I make sure that I am talking to him or her, making sure that I am managing my stress well; I am managing my time well, and that also that I am doing the things necessary in order to maintain mental, physical and spiritual health and wellbeing. I think another thing is also connecting with people who share your interest and can share some of your stress load, and can help alleviate by providing those safe and encouraging and affirming spaces. I think of those as being very important. Even if you know doing certain behaviours that you attribute to being healthy are more well or more whole, finding those people and connecting with those people who do those type of things so as to build the habits and the behaviours necessary to create enduring or sustainable health is not easy.

KB: I think that is a really good question. As a graduate student, have you been successfully able to find those people, as a Black graduate student at a predominately white institution, have you been able to find those people to connect with?

INT-2: Not as much as I like to.

KB: OK.

INT-2: I think part of it is just that, all of us are just so overwhelmed and stressed that when we do get any extra time, we don't want to be structured because so much of our lives are so structured.

KB: *Yeah, yeah.*

INT-2: I think that the other part is that there are some real divisions, even in the Black graduate population.

KB: *Absolutely.*

INT-2: Be they real or perceived, that makes it difficult to build community. And those are things that I think, you know they have an impact.

KB: *Right, Right, right.*

INT-2: On physical health, mental health. And even what are the activities that we pursue when we get together. Are we getting together to eat a whole bunch of unhealthy food? Are we getting together to drink? Are we getting to stay up very late hours? Or are we getting ready to go to church, to do community service, to have a conversation about mental health, are we going for a bike ride? So, when you think about it, that why it's important who you get in touch with and who you build community with, what is in the community . . .

KB: *OK.*

INT-2: And what does the community do?

KB: *It's that people take on different identities in these spaces? Does identity ever come up?*

INT-2: Identity comes up significantly. I think there is real and perceived identity. And there is also intended identity, which is a third one. So, the real identity, these are the markers that are salient that folks know about. So, everyone will know that I am a Black man. Perceived identity is that they will perceive that I am this or I am that or I have to be . . . or that I am poor or that I am wealthy or that I am intelligent. That's a perceived identity. An intended identity, I would imagine, are those I want people to look at me and see this thing. I want them to look at me and see that I am well-adjusted, that I am powerful, that I'm these things. I think identity, you know what we project, what we perceive about ourselves and what we intended to project are huge when it comes to building that community, particularly within Black graduate students. I think that it's a lot of what divide us. When you look at HBCU folks vs. predominately white institutions alums, Greeks vs. non-Greeks, Christians who are active in Church vs. non-Christians, who are not active with a religious organization, loners vs. extroverts. What does it look to people who drink vs. people who don't drink? All of these different identity markers that, when unbalanced, sort of create distance and barriers.

KB: *Thanks. This is really, really good. This is really going to create/showcase how identity impacts our community and how it impacts our health. I like how you describe how identities divide the Black community in spaces such as this. But how does Black identity fit in these spaces? How does a graduate student here, your identity in majority white spaces, does that impact health in any way?*

INT-2: Yes, it does. Because many people . . . Black people are very rarely allowed to be anything more than just Black. So, think about it, intersectionality was something that was born out of Black feminism and Black womanism. The idea that I am more than just a Black person; I'm a Black male who comes from an HBCU and who is an educator. Like there are all of these different things that are very salient parts of my identity, but in many cases it still down to just being Black.

KB: Mm hm.

INT-2: So, part of the work that've I even done with diversity is trying to figure out how we can empower people to choose their most salient identity marker rather than having it imposed on them.

KB: Wow, OK.

INT-2: I think in many cases; some Black women want just be women. Some Black men just want to be a Black male, they want to be Black. Some people . . . and even looking at how the most salient identity marker causes conflict with additional identity markers. So, if my most salient identity marker is being Black and male but also there is an identity marker of being a LBGTQ community, the conflict of being Black and male, Black and female, and Black and Christian, and all of these things, those things being [in] conflict has [a] negative impact on mental, emotional, spiritual and physical health.

KB: Wow!

INT-2: They take a toll. They lead to unhealthy coping mechanisms. When we think of hypersexuality and the comparison factor of always looking at those things, it is critically important to make sure that we are supporting people in what it looks when those . . . when those identities are in conflict, coping mechanisms emerge. Coping mechanisms are not always healthy. So, if your coping mechanisms are couched in conflicting identities, then it may lead to overeating, oversexualizing, overcommitting, not taking care of yourself, not providing or taking care of yourself . . . those are things I think about.

KB: *Thank you for sharing that. Do you have any extra activities to improve your health? Pretty much you summarize that, but I don't know if you had anything else?*

INT-2: No.

KB: *OK. Just for the record, the activities that you do are exercising, dietician, mental health therapist and workout?*

INT-2: Yep, yep, yep.

KB: When you do those activities, do they help improve your health?

INT-2: They do. They help me feel better.

KB: OK. Alright. The last question: if you were asked to help people improve their health, what would you do? And you can specify which group of people, if you want to focus on graduate students or Black graduate students. Whichever group of people.

INT-2: So, I think if I want to help improve Black graduate students' health, I would want to start with the GREATEST threat. Think about the different kinds of health: mental, emotional, spiritual, physical. I think about the two most important places where if you attack these places, it'll have the impact. I think about mental health and emotional health. I think there are a lot of places where we haven't unpacked. There are societal impacts about the intersectionality, the identities being in conflict, that create emotional, intellectual and mental health issues that trickle down into physical health issues. I think a lot of us overeat, we don't eat right, our relationships are in [a] shambles. When you have an impact there and you stabilize people emotionally and mentally, I think that is the first step towards getting someone to a physical health outcome. I think the first thing I would do; I would say, look, you need [to] sit down and see a therapist, advisor and a dietician. Those are first three things that I think that people, particularly Black graduate students, need to do.

KB: OK.

INT-2: And have that check-in to see how you are doing mentally, how you are doing from a time management perspective, what your day to day looks like, and what you are putting into your body in terms of what you will have in terms of 'fuel to endure'.

KB: Thank you for that. You mention the word 'therapist', so I want to go into that. For the therapist here, do you recommend or have you attended CAPS, or are you talking about . . . ?

INT-2: CAPS.

KB: OK.

INT-2: Counselling and Psychological Services.

KB: Have you heard about the other centre, the Center for Human Growth this year?

INT-2: I have. The reason why I recommend CAPS is because there are two Black . . . I like sending people to people. It's about lenses. It's about perspective. If we don't have, we don't share the salient identity marker, it's going to be difficult for me to FEEL like I, what I'm sharing with you is something that you can understand and process.

KB: No, absolutely. OK. Is there anything else you would like to share?

INT-2: No that is it.

KB: Thank you so much for your time.

Lessons Learned

From the above narratives, we learn that for the narrators, such activities as sleeping, eating, and walking re-energize the body, mind and soul. With respect to eating, Interviewee 1 contends that what is eaten is considered 'food' if and only if it is something close to what is cooked at one's home. Eating something just to keep going negatively impacts one's health. Both narrators saw gym and yoga exercising and seeing a dietician for guidance on healthy eating as ways to improve their health. Thus, even though they have little time for real exercise, they believe it is as helpful as eating the right healthy food in terms of boosting their health. On work and leisure, the narrators note that the amount of work one has to do also influences one's health and having free time from work is equally impactful on one's health.

Both narrators speak about Black students studying in a predominantly white institution where identity becomes an issue that significantly influences one's health. They note that building community within the larger community could be difficult due to divisions within the student body. They speak of identity, real and perceived/imagined, as coming up significantly within the IUB community. Identity, they argue, impacts the students' health. As Interviewee 2 noted forcefully: 'Black people are very rarely allowed to be anything more than just Black.' However, he draws attention to the fact that they should be allowed to choose their most salient identity marker rather than having it imposed on them. The most salient identity marker, he noted, could cause conflict with additional identity markers that are either tagged on to them or that they take on. For example, Interviewee 2 stated that 'multiple conflicting identities [such] as being Black, male/female, a part of the LBGTQ community, Christian, etc., often create conflict from the philosophical and practical perspective, and consequently negatively impact one's mental, emotional, spiritual, intellectual and physical health. This, we learn, could lead to unhealthy coping mechanisms and consequently to overeating, oversexualizing, overcommitting and not taking care of one's self'. Still on the subject of community, the narrators noted that even though talking to people within one's group to see how they are keeping healthy is a healthy and beneficial practice, in Bloomington, this is hardly available, given that the university is a predominantly white university. Whatever the circumstances, both narrators strongly advocate the need for people to connect with those who share their interests and to learn from one another.

Furthermore, both narrators spoke forcefully about the need to have quiet time for oneself. Having improper accommodation that does not meet the needs of students, especially where students must share space and facilities, which creates emotional valence, stress and frustration. This, they noted, negatively impacts their health.

Another important issue raised by the narrators is the need for counselling and psychological services for Black people. Both narrators saw mental health and emotional health as being the two most important areas in need of help and/or improvement as far as Black people are concerned. They mentioned the Center for Human Growth and CAPS as centres where Black people can reliably access mental and emotional health help and from which they can benefit. Interviewee 1 also spoke of the relevance of water and sun for physical, spiritual and mental rejuvenation.

Finally, we learned about time management and how that also affects one's health. Specifically, the narrators noted that knowing that one is doing the things that are necessary in order to maintain one's mental, physical and spiritual health and wellbeing is crucial and can only be done effectively if one manages one's time appropriately.

Kourtney Ayanna Dorqual Byrd is a public health practitioner with specialization in community-based participatory research as well as qualitative and quantitative research methods. She engages in community-based participatory research in inner cities and rural Indiana to improve evidence-based programmes and policies. She also works in the area of urban and rural community organizations and structures through evaluation sustenance, translating public health research into feasible policy, and analysing and implementing equitable social policies with a view to improving the health of minority populations.

References

Clark, R., N.B. Anderson, V.R. Clark and David R. Williams. 1999. 'Racism as a Stressor for African Americans: A Biopsychosocial Model'. *American Psychologist* 54(10): 805–16.

Guiffrida, Douglas, A., and Kathryn Z. Douthit. 2010. 'The Black student Experience at Predominantly White Colleges: Implications for School and College Counselors', *Journal of Counseling & Development* 88(3): 311–18.

Krogstad, Jens Manuel, and Richard Fry. 2014. 'More Hispanics, Blacks Enrolling in College, But Lag in Bachelor's Degrees'. Retrieved 19 May 2020 from http://www.pewresearch.org/fact-tank/2014/04/24/more-hispanics-blacks-enrolling-in-college-but-lag-in-bachelors-degrees.

US Commission on Civil Rights. 2010. *The Educational Effectiveness of Historically Black Colleges and Universities, Washington, DC: US Commission on Civil Rights*. Retrieved 21 June 2018 from https://files.eric.ed.gov/fulltext/ED513988.pdf.

Whittaker, Valene A., and Helen Neville. A. 2010. 'Examining the Relation between Racial Identity Attitude Clusters and Psychological Health Outcomes in African American College Students', *Journal of Black Psychology* 36(4): 383–409.

Conclusion

Samuel Gyasi Obeng and Cecilia Sem Obeng

The discursive constructions related to physical health, homelessness and being minority in this volume have brought together diverse disciplines ranging from public health, informatics, and language and linguistic science, especially discourse/conversation analysis. The intersection and entwining of the above-mentioned disciplines help us to understand the plight of vulnerable populations and what their caregivers go through while assisting them. The narratives of the studied participants also help us to understand the expectations of the vulnerable populations and their advocates or caregivers in their attempts to obtain optimal health and social justice. The narratives also provide us with insights into the studied populations' access to healthcare and social recognition. One thing that the narratives have in common is their provision of a window or glimpse into the lived experiences of certain vulnerable populations from their unique perspectives. Specifically, through their narratives we were led into the physical and/or socioemotional health that these storytellers dealt with daily, their access to (or denial of) health and justice, the constructs of privilege and positionality that impact their daily lives, and their being singled out as 'other' by mainstream society. These, we saw, created a situation that made it impossible to have a level playing field in terms of social, financial and other dimensions of health. The above roadblocks also impeded the studied participants' acceptance and inclusion into mainstream society and, hence, access to equal opportunities in relation to whatever resources society had, among other things.

One thing is clear from all the narratives: people develop strategies to deal with their unique social and psychological situations and with their physical, social, financial, emotional and even environmental health. What is not lost in all these narratives is the fact that those with unique health challenges are not alone in their pursuit of access to social justice and for justice in accessing healthcare; their caregivers and advocates also deal with their unique circumstances in caring for them. Thus, even though their social justice and healthcare journeys may clash and blend, there is a will, and hence a way, to find solutions that they hope will keep them afloat in life's swift currents and thus help them attain some form of healthy living, even when the provision of a pathway to optimal health is encumbered or limited. For those who felt excluded from the mainstream because of homelessness and ethnicity, the situation was the same. Hope and determination emboldened and encouraged them to seek social justice and to better their lot, despite the numerous roadblocks placed on the paths of their life journeys.

On the healthcare access experiences of a group that is often overlooked, even ignored, the group we prefer to label as 'New Americans', who are often wrongly referred to as 'immigrants' despite being naturalized as US citizens, we hear stories of denial, uncertainty, insults and entrapment. Via their narratives, we see how language and discourse narratives unveil valency in the synthesis and analysis of issues that confront them and that they must overcome in order to live as normal human beings. There is no doubt that living on the margins of a society, whose healthcare system and ethnic boundaries are as prickly as double-edged, razor-sharp swords, is tricky and requires courage, the will to survive and a determination to keep one's head above water, the strength of whose tides only the brave can manoeuvre through to safety.

We discovered that the content, context, co-text and intertext of the narrators' stories were encouraging and were themselves pathways to strong, enduring and successful character building. They struggle daily to barely survive, but the light they catch a glimpse of at the end of the struggling tunnel of their lives, even if dim, is enough to act as a morale-booster to keep them striving ahead. Their domicile ecologies as well as their discursive ecologies are emblematic and revealing of their courage and optimism in the face of sickness, poverty, rejection and possible death.

We discovered further that for some of the participants, such as the homeless, their social, familial (kinship, including those acquired on the street to help keep them alive and maintain their sanity) and healthcare providers (a uniquely acquired relation) all impact their person, personality, mind, soul and spirit. They lean on and highlight these networks, and amplify the singularly important role each plays in their lives. There is pluralism and interdependence even though they also experience individualism and loneliness every now and then. Their daily living, we discovered, constitutes contests, wits, sheer determination and cooperation with people they must work with, become friends with, yield to, ever so often overrun and, yes, sometimes ignore in order for life to continue.

An important lesson we learn from these narratives is that society, government, sociocultural actors, healthcare providers and all stakeholders must not only listen to the concerns expressed in the narrators' stories, but must also pay attention to these stories because the anecdotes are full of holes in the lives of the narrators – lacunas that require being filled with encouragement, unrestricted love, provision of care in all dimensions of health (physical, spiritual, environmental, social, emotional, financial, occupational and intellectual) and acceptance. Inattention to the narrators' needs and pleas for help can render their modes of communication, their needs and their survivorship useless and ineffectual, and can cause them to fall off life's treacherous cliff.

The narratives also revealed the entwining between language, power, ideology, justice, healthcare access and healthcare delivery, given how actors with power decide on policies that affect the lives of these nonpowerful ordinary citizens. Our narrators may have chosen to or may have been forced to live on the street, take care of the needy or even emigrate to the United States, but the absence of a listening ear to hear their lives' tremors and an official caring heart to mitigate their plight entrap them in ecologies that perpetuate their precarious conditions and make upward mobility an imaginary and hence unfulfilled dream. The crosscurrents in their stories shed light on a gambit of themes that run through such stories to help readers to share their perspective. Thus, through the tone and tenor of their stories, we are able to inspect their joy, sorrow, plight, fights, surrenders and mood, thereby enabling us to ascertain the authenticity of their stories and of their lives.

These wonderful individuals are human beings like the rest of society. They breathe the same air that the so-called mainstream breathes, think about life in the same way that the mainstream does, and fight to survive just as mainstreamers do, despite operating from a biased, hidden and neglected ecology that continues to mute their voices – voices society must hear in order to join hands with them to create a better survivable living condition for them to work within. There is authenticity and credence in their voices. Society must therefore help unmute their voices so that we, as a people, can listen, hear and act accordingly.

An important question the contributors posed to each of the narrators was why they chose to tell them their stories, and the responses received were strikingly similar, if not identical. In particular, each narrator wanted the world to hear their 'voice'; that is, their unique condition, their plight, how they see society as perceiving them, their desire to be allowed to participate in their own affairs and in the affairs of their families and communities like everyone else, and the resources they needed to function. There was less emphasis on being given 'handouts' or being taken care of; rather, they wanted to be resourced in order to function and compete like everyone else. They detested intrusion of their personal liberties by society via labelling, resource denial or curtailment that resulted in their seeking shelter or survival from social services and/or being at the mercy of certain individuals.

What sets the narratives apart was the fact that each narrator had a different and/or unique disability or sociopolitical problem. A participant who was a naturalized US citizen had to deal with her daughter being bullied at school. The participant who was African American spoke about discrimination and negative societal perception about his ethnicity and how this impacted his socioemotional, financial and other health dimensions. For those caring for the disabled, such as the doctor caring for the deaf person in Chapter 3, their unique challenge was gaining the trust of the clients and learning to communicate competently with them in order to offer them the most effective care, as well as the emotional burden of ensuring recovery and optimal health for their clients. For those who suffered from a form of illness, their unique challenge was acceptance, the availability of tools for recovery and the elimination of any form of intrusion on both their positive and negative liberties (Berlin 1969; Obeng 2018, 2020). For the homeless, the challenge was acceptance, violence and denial of basic rights. Their inability to access appropriate services and what they saw as a forced perpetuity to directly and indirectly appeal to social services (shelter officials, etc.) for help created an indelible sense of shame and disillusionment for them. Thus, their special condition (for example, that of homelessness) constituted a face-threat, curtailing their desire to fight for their freedom to lead normal lives. Also, homelessness put them in jeopardy in terms of the judicial system. In particular, their homelessness and its accompanying problems with the court system, a system that Hannah Kelling (Chapter 1) succinctly described as operating 'on a guilty-until-proven-innocent basis' and in which 'judges had their minds made up long before the trial began', led to stigmatization and an intrusion into their negative and positive liberty (Berlin 1969), and, consequently, a denial of their ability to access real justice.

A principal contribution made by this book is the unmuting of voices of some members of the vulnerable populations in the United States and those of their caregivers and advocates. The stories have revealed the uniqueness as well as the commonalities or the overlapping health needs of each population and their desire to seek optimal health. From these voices, we learned about how they dealt with their plight and the insatiable hope that carried them through life's currents. Common themes that run across the gamut of the narratives were determination, hope, courage and, sometimes, rebellion. They knew that they had a fighting chance, even if verbally, and so they persevered by seeking justice, relevant help and, for the homeless, negotiating 'kinship' and 'families' by bonding with other people in the same 'boat' as them and riding together against and through life's strong currents. They knew about and expected obstacles in their path, so they prepared themselves to face these with all their might. For those with various illnesses, the way out, we discovered, was to take advantage of every opportunity by attending their clinics and meeting with their doctors, following their doctors' advice and recommendations, and making sure that what was due to them in terms of medication and therapies was available and wisely used. For the minorities, an important way of dealing with their unique circumstances was to ignore negative attitudes and comments, and to work hard in every facet of their lives to improve their lot and to do well. For caseworkers and healthcare providers, the balance of professional care delivery and empathy were pivotal to ensuring success. They also had to negotiate appropriate barriers to avoid becoming burnt out.

We also learned from these narratives that despite life being difficult, there were a few occasions when the narrators felt like 'regular' and/or 'normal' human beings. The naturalized US citizen's child was accepted by her schoolmates after participating in a TV programme; the homeless person felt at home in the company of other homeless people and on occasions when he had access to his son. The ataxia sufferers spoke positively about their caregivers (family and health professionals) and the deaf person felt loved at times despite being frustrated most of the time. They each saw some goodness (and badness of course) in people and took comfort in the fact that all was not lost and that with public education, things might improve for them.

From the narratives, some moral lessons can be drawn. First, it is incumbent on society to 'open' its eyes and be familiar with its social, political and cultural ecologies, as well as how these ecologies impact healthcare access and healthcare delivery. Society must take note of the fact that disability, in whatever form, does not equal inability. Despite their perceived disadvantage, we discovered that most of the narrators were successful because they did not see failure as an option. They were hopeful and therefore empowered themselves because they believed in fighting to win against all odds, and hence succeeded in ways in which some so-called mainstreamers would have failed. Despite open verbal attacks and discrimination, the minorities did not perish; they persevered. If society familiarized itself with its ecology and acted responsibly towards these narrators, not only will life become more bearable for them, it will create social harmony between us all.

Second, medical schools could expand their curriculum on communication to include communication with the hearing impaired and people with other health needs that require knowledge of unique verbal and nonverbal communication. Teaching physicians communicative strategies for breaking good and bad news (Maynard 2003; Maynard and Freese 2012; Obeng 2018) will enhance their level of communicative competence and consequently will help to improve physician–client interaction in particular and caregiving as a whole.

Third, it is incumbent on governments, states, local communities and all stakeholders to join together to fight racism, xenophobia and other forms of discrimination. Paying lip service to or adopting a wait-and-see attitude in terms of dealing with these and other social problems that threaten the free participation of people in their social, familial, and personal lives can result in vulnerable populations experiencing bitterness and a perception of rejection. Imagining ourselves in the place of each of the participants affords us the opportunity to listen, learn and come up with workable solutions.

Fourth, society must provide the necessary physical and infrastructural resources as well as the necessary educational facilities so that people can place themselves in the narrators' shoes in order to consequently help these narrators and those like them overcome any hindrances or obstacles placed in their paths, either intentionally or unintentionally. It helps no one, especially not such vulnerable populations, if society expects them to do well and be successful when the relevant resources are withheld from them and their caregivers, or if society keeps resources away from minorities and then complains that they are not pulling their weight. Competing on an equal footing with mainstreamers will give minorities confidence and will boost their competitive spirit. This will be good for them and for the entire population.

Finally, if we believe in Thomas Jefferson's (1776) words – 'We hold these truths to be self-evident, that all men are created equal. That they are endowed by their Creator with certain unalienable Rights, that among these are Life, Liberty, and the pursuit of Happiness' – in the declaration of US independence, then society must prevent or avoid acts that prevent anyone from pursuing life, liberty and happiness. Society must put in place strategies for providing optimal health and protection of vulnerable populations, and the resources needed by such populations to live decent lives. Society must also ensure the liberty of one and all to the extent that vulnerable populations and the people working with them will not feel excluded from public discourse and from participation in decisions that affect their lives and those of others. Furthermore, society must avoid any act or behaviour that jeopardizes such populations' chances of competing fairly for opportunities that come their way. From the narratives, we observe a strong determination on the part of members of vulnerable populations to overcome their current health predicament and all associated encumbrances on their quality of life. Their desire for legitimacy comes across loud and clear, as is a recognition of their unique profile. They detest being recipients of handouts from mainstream society. On the contrary, the narrators strive to develop their own resources via their own means, even if such means are insufficient. Indeed, the desire of each narrators for the recognition of their negative liberty and positive liberty is explicitly stated. Like everyone else, they strive for normality and seek as much latitude as is available to so-called mainstream society so that they can obtain access to whatever resources exist in society. It is therefore incumbent on society to ensure that vulnerable populations are never denied happiness; any act that puts them in a situation that makes them unhappy must be removed swiftly and permanently so as not to worsen their situation. Social services, law enforcement, family and communities must be educated on the liberties of such populations to ensure that such liberties are restored and enforced. Vulnerable populations must be protected from violence, discrimination, bullying and neglect, and must be listened to because they are the best people to come up with solutions for the problems in their lived experiences. They know and understand their situations best, so not involving them in ways that will help them overcome their problems is not only condescending, it is plainly wrong and immoral.

Samuel Gyasi Obeng is a tenured full Professor of Linguistics at Indiana University-Bloomington. He is also an affiliated faculty of Indiana University-Bloomington's Hutton Honors College and the African Studies Program (which he directed from 2007 to 2015) in the Hamilton Lugar School of Global and International Studies. He has published thirty books, over 150 papers in refereed journals and book chapters, and twenty-five book and article reviews. He was also the editor-in-chief of *Africa Today, Issues in Intercultural Communication* and *Issues in Political Discourse Analysis*.

Cecilia Sem Obeng is a tenured Associate Professor in the Department of Applied Health Science at Indiana University-Bloomington's School of Public Health, Bloomington. She is an established scholar in the field of children's health and has published six books. She is the author of over sixty peer-reviewed publications. She has provided over a hundred academic/professional and scientific presentations at conferences and has also been an invited speaker. She has spent several years undertaking community-based research in African American communities and publishing her findings in peer-reviewed journals. She has mentored over fifty students to present papers at national and international conferences.

References

Berlin, Isaiah. 1969. *Four Essays on Liberty*. Oxford: Oxford University Press.
Jefferson, Thomas. 1776. 'The Declaration of Independence: The Want, Will, and Hopes of the People'. Retrieved 14 May 2020 from http://www.ushistory.org/Declaration/document
Maynard, Douglas. 2003. *Bad News, Good News: Conversational Order in Everyday Talk and Clinical Settings*. Chicago: University of Chicago Press.
Maynard, Douglas, and Jeremy Freese. 2012. 'Good News, Bad News, and Affect: Practical and Temporal "Emotion Work" in Everyday Life', in Anssi Perakyla and Marja-Leena Sorjonen (eds), *Emotion in Interaction*. Oxford: Oxford University Press, pp. 11–29.
Obeng, Samuel Gyasi. 2018. 'Language and Liberty in Ghanaian Political Communication: A Critical Discourse Perspective', *Ghana Journal of Linguistics* 7(2): 199–224.
———. 2019. 'Language and Liberty in the Ghanaian Political Ecology: An Overview', in Samuel Gyasi Obeng and Emmanuel Debrah (eds), *Ghanaian Politics and Political Communication*. New York: Rowman & Littlefield, pp. 211–24.
———. 2020. 'Grammatical Pragmatics: Language, Power and Liberty in African (Ghanaian) Political Discourse', *Discourse and Society* 31(1): 85–104.

Epilogue

Samuel Gyasi Obeng

After we sat with the Hitherto Invisible Faces,
And listened to their Hitherto Imperceptible Stories,
We realized how Foolish
We as a Society have become!
After all, their Faces had always been Visible
It was us, the so-called Mainstream, who refused to recognize them
We were the ones whose faces were invisible to them because we avoided them
We were the ones who muted their Voices
We, indeed, were the ones who muted their Stories

Their stories were emblematic of Sorrow, Resilience, and Courage
Often associated with People who journey through life with Courage
They may have some of Life's most different and difficult experiences
Yet, they woke up daily knowing there was a fight to be fought
Yet, they woke up daily ready to fight knowing there was a glimmer of Hope
Hope is what saw them through in their daily routines
Hope is what informed their actions and battle-cry
Hope is what made them reach out for help if it was available
Hope is what made them pull through even when they saw themselves in the Minority
Hope indeed is what made them have Optimism rather than Despair

As we packed bags and baggage to go back to our own places of abode,
We said to one another:
It was worth it!
It was worth our time!

It was, indeed, worth Their Time!
They taught us Life's Lessons
That we could learn from them only
They taught us Wisdom about Life and Living
That we could receive from Nowhere other than from Them
They taught us Humility
That we could neither buy with Silver nor Gold.

We pondered over the Wealth of Life Treasure They had given us
We wondered whether we should keep it in our hearts only
We contemplated whether we should keep it in our minds only
We deliberated among ourselves whether we should keep it among ourselves only
Then we were reminded of the Good Old Saying about what motivated our exploration
Then we were reminded of what prompted our investigation, our desire for knowledge
Then we realized how unfortunate it would be if we did not share with the rest of the world!

As messengers,
We went to the field
As messengers, we collected our 'News'
As messengers, we delivered our News
As messengers, we brought Their Responses
As messengers, we scribed Their Pain
As messengers, we scribed Their Courage
As messengers, we scribed Their Joy in Sharing their Stories with us
As messengers, we were Loved by Them and we Loved them Back
We hope Those who have Ears have Heard Them and will act accordingly
We hope when push comes to shove, Eyes, Ears, and Policy will work in concert
We hope that someday, the Voices of One and All will be Listened to
We hope that someday the Faces of One and All will be given an equitable opportunity in Visibility
Yes, we hope!
Yes, we believe!
Yes, we yearn for!
Yes! Yes! And; Yes!

INDEX

Aday, Luu Aann, 10, 18
Affordable Care Act, 11, 93, 105
African American, 13, 17, 110–117, 124–132
Afro-Caribbean, 13, 15, 115–117, 122
American Community Survey (ACS), 93, 114
American Sign Language (ASL), 7, 66, 82–83, 91
Americans with Disabilities Act (ADA), 7, 9, 18, 68, 81, 83
Asian American, 116
ataxia, ix, 3, 6–7, 45–65, 137

Batalova, Jeanne, 93–94, 114
Berlin, Isaiah, 3, 18, 136, 140
Black and Brown, 115
black feminism, 128
Black Graduate Student Association of Indiana University 14, 115
black identity, 13, 14, 15, 115, 128
black womanism, 16, 128
Bloomington, 10–18, 19, 22, 26, 90, 92–96, 101, 104–107, 111–116, 130, 139
Boko Haram, 12, 93, 103
bullying, 13, 113, 139

caregiver, 19, 45, 56, 100, 133–138
caseworker, 4–5, 44, 137
Center for Human Growth, 119–120, 129, 131
children of deaf adults (CODAs), 69
civil rights, 9, 14, 18, 68, 91, 116, 132
Clark, R., 116, 131

and N.B. Anderson and David R. Williams, 116, 131
communication disorder, 7, 68, 90
Counseling and Psychological Services (CAPS), 120, 129, 131
Current Population Survey (CPS), 93, 114

deaf, 7–10, 17, 66–91, 136–137
deafness, ix
Deaf, 7–10, 66–91
Derose, Kathryn Pitkin, 94, 114
disability, 63, 71, 90, 136–137
diversity, 128

Ehrmann, Max, 66, 90, 91
Escarce, José J., 94, 114
Evansville, 4, 23

Flaskerud, Jacquelyn, 10, 18
Freese, Jeremy, 138, 140
Garrett, Katherine, 10, 18

hard of hearing, viii–ix, 7, 8–10, 66, 68–69, 71, 78, 91
Hausa, 13, 109–110
health, ix–x, 1–3, 5, 10–11, 14, 17, 45, 51, 77, 78, 86–87, 92–93, 96, 98–100, 102–106, 114, 116–118, 121–123, 126–128, 130–133, 138
cultural health, 1
emotional health, ix–x, 1, 3, 12, 13, 15, 113–114, 128, 138
environmental health, ix, 1, 3, 6, 12, 17, 113, 133, 135, 138

financial health, ix–x, 1, 3, 5, 10–12, 17, 92–94, 113–114, 133–136
holistic health, 115, 119
intellectual health, 16, 129–130, 135
mental health, ix, 1, 3, 5, 10, 13–16, 28, 30, 40–42, 53, 56, 93, 100–102, 113, 115–116, 118, 124–1301
occupational health, 132, 138
public health, 1, 11, 17, 67–68, 90, 94, 103, 114, 116, 125, 131, 133, 139
physical health, ix, 10, 13, 15–16, 95, 115, 119, 125–126, 128, 130, 133, 138
social health, ix, 1, 3, 10, 11–13, 17, 92–94, 113, 133, 135
spiritual health, ix, 1, 10, 13, 16, 92–94, 113, 115, 118–119, 126, 128–131, 135
healthcare, 1–3, 6–10, 12, 15, 17, 39, 41, 44, 66, 68–69, 78–80, 85, 88–90, 93–94, 98, 100–101, 106, 113, 114, 133–135, 137
health communication, 9
health discourse, 9
health insurance, 5, 9, 11, 15, 38–41, 85, 98, 100–103, 106, 122–123
health (care) provider, 2–3, 8, 17, 66, 69, 80–81, 84, 86–89, 101, 134, 135, 137
hearing impaired, 3, 8–9, 71, 74, 137
Hispanic, 116, 131
Historically Black Colleges and Universities (HBCU), 116, 127–128, 132
homeless, 2–5, 17, 19–44, 13–134, 136–137

immigrants, x, 3, 10–11, 18, 92, 94, 102–103, 113–114, 134
Informatics, 65, 133

Jefferson, Thomas, 17–18, 138, 140
Jones, Mackenzie, 7–9, 66, 70, 81, 90
Jordan, 11, 92–97
Jordanian, 10, 92–93, 97, 113

Kelling, Hannah, 3–5, 32, 44, 136
Kittaneh, Ema, 10–13, 93, 95, 103, 114
Kresnye, Cassie, 6, 46, 56, 66

LBGTQ, 128, 130
liberty, 18, 136, 138–140
    negative liberty, 136, 139
    positive liberty, 136, 139
Lurie, Nicole, 94, 114

Maynard, Douglas, 138, 140
Middle East, 94
Montana Disability and Health Program, 90
Morris County, 23

Nigeria, 12–13, 93, 103–110
    Nigerian, 12–13, 93, 108, 110, 113

Obeng, Cecilia Sem, 17, 139
Obeng, Samuel Gyasi, 3, 18, 136, 138–140
Orange County, 4, 23
otolaryngology, 67

physical activity, 12, 15–16, 55, 95, 107, 113, 115, 125

Quran, 103

racial stressors, 13, 15, 116
Rizer, Sarah L., 82, 91

shelter (homeless shelter), 4, 20, 21, 23–26, 29–31, 36, 40–41, 136
social worker, 5, 20, 37
Southern Indiana, 4
stress, 7, 13, 15–16, 101, 126, 131

stressful tasks, 16, 116
stressor, 13, 15, 116

US Commission on Civil Rights, 14, 19, 68, 91, 116, 132
US Department of Justice, 68, 91

video relay system (VRS), 8, 11, 66, 76–77, 87, 91

video remote interpreting (VRI), 9, 85, 87, 89, 91
vulnerable populations, 1–2, 11, 17–18, 94, 114, 133, 136, 138–139

Winslow, Betty, 10, 18

YMCA, 10, 92, 95

www.ingramcontent.com/pod-product-compliance
Lightning Source LLC
Chambersburg PA
CBHW071713020426
42333CB00017B/2256